Praise for *Don't Go to Bed Angry: Stay Up and Fight!*

"*Don't Go to Bed Angry: Stay Up and Fight*! packs a one-two punch into the gut of all marital conflict no matter the source. The book is both transparent and practical, offering couples a variety of proven tools to develop marital muscles to knock out every opponent and arise as Christlike champions. An incredible resource!"

—**Clint and Penny A. Bragg**, authors of *Marriage on the Mend—
Healing Your Relationship After Crisis, Separation, or Divorce*
and founders, Inverse Ministries

"In *Don't Go To Bed Angry: Stay Up and Fight!* Deb and Ron DeArmond deliver a biblically based book on the topic of marital conflict. Practical exercises will help the reader move away from the potential damage conflict can bring to the discovery that comes from learning to stand together as allies not enemies—even when you don't see eye to eye. We highly recommend this book as a creative guide for any couple at any stage of life to find alignment with each other—and God—in their marriage."

—**Claudia & David Arp**, co-authors, *10 Great Dates to Energize Your
Marriage* and founders, Marriage Alive International

"*Don't Go to Bed Angry* has a solid biblical foundation and is full of wise counsel and great practical tools. Deb and Ron are open and honest as they share from their experiences and those of others. I have been counseling couples for over thirty years, and this great, new title goes immediately to the top of my list of books on how to deal with conflict in marriage and grow your marriage God's way."

—**Kim Kimberling, PhD**, author of *Seven Secrets to an Awesome
Marriage* and leader of the Awesome Marriage Movement

"Deb DeArmond has done it again, this time with the help of her husband! Together they get all in your business and deal with real marriage struggles, touch on sensitive relational issues, and give you the right tools to build a healthy relationship. Pick up this book if you want to fight for a good marriage, punch division in the face, and win together in life! It's time to put on your gloves and get to work on a great marriage!"

—**Amy Schafer**, Co-Lead Pastor at Grace Life Church and host,
Cornerstone Television Network

"There are not enough resources that talk about honest, creative, and relevant conflict resolution. We believers typically avoid conflict or simply pretend that it doesn't exist because 'we are supposed to have all the answers.' In their new book, *Don't Go to Bed Angry: Stay Up and Fight!*, Deb and Ron bring the issue into the light and give couples real stories and real tools to bring about real peace. The Hendersons need the help found in this book, and so do you!"

—**Paige and Richard Henderson**, founders, Fellowship of the Sword, www.fellowshipofthesword.com

"Wow! Deb DeArmond and her husband, Ron, hit the ball out of the park with their new book on marriage. As I read, it was as if a wise mentor couple sat across from me, generously sharing their hard-won wisdom. Couples who read the book will find godly instruction, helpful tools, and personal stories. Each chapter is chock-full of the kinds of things I wish my husband and I had known before we walked the aisle. If you're married—or about to be—don't learn the hard way; read (and apply) the practical advice in the DeArmonds' book!"

—**Dena Dyer**, author, speaker, and musician, *25 Christmas Blessings: An Inspiring Countdown to Christmas*

"When my sons were teenagers, they often argued. Finally one day, I sat them on our couch and said, 'I'm going to teach you how to fight.' They were shocked. They thought they were *experts*. I gave a couple of steps to keep their arguments respectful and to help them own their own feelings. In their book, the DeArmonds have set us all down on their own couch and given us the principles to do *right* what we probably all do, and do wrong. These principles work! The sooner you start, the sooner you reap the benefits."

—**Joann Cole Webster**, Vice President, Christian Men's Network

"In our work with couples in crisis for twenty years, we have seen the value of having conflict resolution skills. 'Fights'—loud and silent—can become long lasting wars with much devastation. In *Don't Go To Bed Angry*, Deb and Ron give us a pattern to develop essential skills to resolve inevitable marital conflict. Read this book and let God guide the application to your marriage. Then you can begin the 'fight for' your marriage. It's so worth it!"

—**Mona Shriver**, author of *Unfaithful* and cofounder, Hope & Healing Ministries

"I love Deb and Ron's honest approach to surviving something we all experience but normally lock behind closed doors—marital conflict. *Don't Go to Bed Angry* provides helpful steps to resolve life's conflicts in a way that actually deepens our marriage."

—**Jonathan McKee**, author of more than 20 books including
52 Ways to Connect with Your Smartphone Obsessed Kid

"We often say that if there's no conflict in your marriage, one of you has disappeared. Ron and Deb DeArmond take that thought several steps further, teaching us that conflict between a couple is not only normal and expected, but that it can be a healthy and helpful part of the relationship! In *Don't Go to Bed Angry*, the DeArmonds have done a masterful job of bringing their own vulnerability as well as years of hard-won wisdom to the table. Through stories, studies, and "hands-on" interactive guides, they show us how learning the art of conflict, confrontation, and resolution can help create stronger and more intimate marriages. We're excited to see how the influence of the DeArmonds and their message will impact generations to come!"

—**Alan and Nancy Smith**, senior pastors, Catch the Fire DFW

"Deb and Ron DeArmond tackle marital conflict in their new book, *Don't Go to Bed Angry: Stay Up and Fight!* Repressed hurts and resentments can fester and build until there's an explosion where you wound the one you love. With eye-opening stories, tips for communication, and rules for fair fights, their book is a valuable resource for couples who want to go through married life as sweethearts instead of angry boxing partners. I highly recommend this book!"

—**Michelle Cox**, author of *Just 18 Summers, God Glimpses from the Jewelry Box* (fall 2016), and *God Glimpses from the Toolbox* (fall 2016)

"We've known and loved Ron and Deb DeArmond and their entire family for over twenty years. We've been eyewitnesses to them working through many of life's difficulties with wisdom and covenant as their approach. Over the past thirty years we have ministered to thousands of men and women, and we could have used this book for every one of them. Now we have a great tool to help guys and gals fix their marriage!"

—**Jack & Betty King**, Faithful Men Ministries

"Somewhere between papering over problems and drawing blood lies common ground where healthy couples handle conflict. Kudos to Deb and Ron DeArmond for teaching us how to find this promised land and build healthy homes on it!"

—**Shellie Rushing Tomlinson**, Belle of All Things Southern and author of *Heart Wide Open*

"More great marital herspective from relationship expert Deb DeArmond, this time including insightful hispective from husband, Ron. They show us how to 'Put on the Gloves' and fight fair within Papa God's strange and beautiful marriage math: 1+1 = 1. Their premise 'Be clear about who the enemy is—and isn't' was a huge help for me. Sure clarifies why it's important for your spouse to be in your corner. On a five-star scale, I give this one six."

—**Debora M. Coty**, speaker and award-winning author of the Too Blessed to be Stressed line of inspirational books, www.DeboraCoty.com

"Funny, insightful, practical, full of wisdom and grace. As a married couple, we are on the same team, fighting the same enemy, pursing the same goal—staying married and glorifying God in the process. Ron and Deb live what they write and share from their years of experience—victories and setbacks—to encourage us all to finish our race triumphantly. Bless them!"

—**Mark and Jill Palmer**, learning to fight fair for 16 years and counting. Lead pastors of River Church in Durango, CO.

Praise for Deb DeArmond's previous book, *I Choose You Today: 31 Choices to Make Love Last*

"It's often been said that our choices define us. That's true personally, but it's also a key to our *relationships*. Deb DeArmond has provided a practical and insightful book detailing 31 choices we can make as husbands and wives that have the potential to transform even a good marriage—and make it a great one."

—**Greg Smalley**, Vice President of Family Ministry, Focus on the Family

DON'T
GO TO BED
ANGRY
Stay Up and Fight

DEB DEARMOND & RON DEARMOND

ABINGDON PRESS

NASHVILLE

DON'T GO TO BED ANGRY
STAY UP AND FIGHT!

Library of Congress Cataloging-in-Publication Data

Names: DeArmond, Deb.
Title: Don't go to bed angry : stay up and fight! / Deb and Ron DeArmond.
Description: First [edition]. | Nashville, Tennessee : Abingdon Press, 2016.
   | Includes bibliographical references.
Identifiers: LCCN 2015037192 (print) | LCCN 2015043630 (ebook) | ISBN
   9781426790935 (binding: pbk. : alk. paper) | ISBN 9781501816406 (e-book)
Subjects: LCSH: Marriage—Religious aspects—Christianity. | Conflict
   management—Religious aspects—Christianity.
Classification: LCC BV835 .D426 2016 (print) | LCC BV835 (ebook) | DDC
   248.8/44—dc23
LC record available at http://lccn.loc.gov/2015037192

16 17 18 19 20 21 22 23—10 9 8 7 6 5 4 3 2 1
MANUFACTURED IN THE UNITED STATES OF AMERICA

Contents

Acknowledgments / xi

Introduction: Rules? There Are Rules? / xiii

Put on the Gloves! Introduction / xxiii

1. What's Wrong with Us? Can't We Just Get Along? / 1

Put on the Gloves! Chapter 1 /7

Burdens

2. Is It Just Us? / 9

Put on the Gloves! Chapter 2 / 17

Baggage

3. Leave That Baggage on the Carousel! / 19

Put on the Gloves! Chapter 3 / 32

Bridges

4. Communication Tools That Work / 35

Put on the Gloves! Chapter 4 / 55

Barriers

5. The Keys to Conflict Styles / 59

Put on the Gloves! Chapter 5 / 75

6. Communication Traps / 77

Put on the Gloves! Chapter 6 / 103

7. Your Past Doesn't Have to Be Your Future / 105
Put on the Gloves! Chapter 7 / 117

BOUNDARIES

8. Rules of Engagement: Learning to Fight Fair / 119
Put on the Gloves! Chapter 8 / 137

BLESSINGS

9. How Do We Get There from Here? / 139
Put on the Gloves! Chapter 9 / 150

Appendix A: Scriptures and Intentions / 153
Appendix B: The Rules / 167
Appendix C: Excerpt from *Got Vision?* / 169
Resources / 177

For Jesus, the victor in the greatest battle.
Seeing us as His prize,
He vanquished the enemy
who was determined to destroy us.

Acknowledgments

From Deb to Ron: Coauthoring this book was a wild and wooly experience. Two heads, two hearts, but only ten fingers, brought many opportunities to practice the principles God's taught us in the last forty years. Tomorrow is *still* ours.

From Ron to Deb: Thank you for being the wife of my youth. From the beginning you've been interested in what my heart has to say, and forty-plus years later that's still true. Thanks for giving my voice a place in your life.

With love to our sons, Cameron, Jordan, and Bryce: you lived through our "formative years" as we learned to build our lives as a couple and as a family. Thanks for your love and patience with the way-less-than-perfect parents God gave you! We love you and are so very proud of you all. You've added the next generation of DeArmonds with your wonderful wives and beautiful sons. We may not have it all together, but together we have it all!

We learned much about marriage from our parents, Larry and Dorothy Graeme and Mel and Virginia Rolin. We paid attention. Thanks for the life lessons.

Our appreciation goes to the folks at Abingdon Press—Ramona

Richards, Cat Hoort, and company. Many thanks are owed to the WordServe Literary family, Alice Bair Crider and Greg Johnson, for their great support and encouragement.

Our special gratitude to all who shared their experiences of marital conflict—the good, the bad, and occasionally, the tragic. Whether through the survey or in conversation, your stories were important as we shaped this work. Thank you.

A special note of thanks to Cindy Smith, Karen DeArmond Gardner, Kathy Carlton Willis, our pastors Alan and Nancy Smith, and so many other dear friends. You are gifts in our lives, and we can't imagine our lives without you in them!

INTRODUCTION
Rules? There Are Rules?

"Yes, I know. Every marriage has conflict," she said. "But *how* do you fight?" The forceful staccato of her words punched the air as she leaned forward in her seat.

I wasn't sure I understood her question, but I noticed every eye in the room was locked on us. My husband looked at me and we grinned at each other. The couples group we were addressing seemed pretty serious, intent on getting some insight.

"Well, occasionally there's a slammed door or two," I began. "Volume may go up, and often the dogs will run out of the room. But we always follow the rules."

The pretty redhead with the puzzled look in the front raised her hand. "Rules? Rules for having an argument?" Absolutely. There had better be rules. It's how we've stayed married and happy for forty years.

The old saying "All's fair in love and war" is baloney. Dangerous stuff. It's a license to put on the gloves, leave kindness (and good judgment) behind, and take no prisoners. All so that you can make your point, snatch the prize, and come out the winner in the moment. But that's the problem with the approach: you may win in the moment and end up sacrificing the life of the relationship.

"So what are your rules?" someone asked.

"They're pretty simple: No name calling, nothing physical (slammed doors aside), no dragging up the past with a 'You always' approach." I paused for a moment. "Oh, and no one is allowed to get in the car and drive off."

Ron picked up the list. "If one of us needs some space and wants time to think or cool off before we continue, we ask permission to take a break with a specific time commitment for returning to the discussion. Another important principle is we don't make a decision about the *thing*, the issue that created the conflict, until all is peaceful."

They were writing this stuff down. I understood. No one handed us the rules when we got married. We had to fight through a lot of unpleasant moments to discover them. And by *unpleasant*, I mean ugly, angry, painful moments. We weren't always proud of how we handled the conflict. And neither was God.

The rules surfaced over time. They kind of revealed themselves through those moments after a difficult interaction when we asked forgiveness from each other—and from God. "It really hurt when you..." or "I was fine up until you..." The debrief was important to help us understand when the conflict stopped being healthy and took on a destructive tone.

And don't misunderstand; we haven't arrived at a perfect record. We sometimes slip back into bad behavior. But there are two principles or truths to which we submit. The first is: *If you have to fight, fight fair.* And the second is even more essential: *be clear about who the enemy is—and isn't.*

There *is* an enemy who has set himself against us because we follow Jesus (see Ephesians 6:12). People—in this case, our mates—are not the enemy. We don't need to target them or engage in the wrong combat. When conflict arises between husband and wife, our awareness must be heightened, and we must be on the alert: *we have a difference*, but we have been given the weapons of warfare to *fight together* against the enemy's attack and resist the temptation to turn on each other. When we stand together, God will lead us to discover His best outcome in the conflict.

Marriage Is a Merger

Our marriage can't be treated as a separate entity from our faith. It is who we are, and it comes with a commitment to become more like Jesus each and every day. It's a mindful, purposeful choice to walk in the Lord as we live out our marriage.

"All's fair in love and war" may sound like a good idea when you need permission to go all in and let it fly. But ask yourself, *Can I really afford that trip—leaving behind my redeemed identity as a follower of Christ and heading to a place of disobedience and destruction and a destiny He poured out His life to prevent?*

Marriage is God's plan; it has been since the beginning. But, it is naive for couples to believe that strong marriages never encounter conflict. The truth is, God's math is tough to add up: 1+1=1. It requires a *merged existence*. The merge has to be about the product of the merger, not the conflict of the process.

Merging requires carving out space (which already sounds like it might hurt a little) for each other if we are to enjoy the supernatural life of unity to which God calls us. It's far more difficult than consolidating his socks and underwear to create a drawer for her lingerie. It's not consolidation that creates space in our hearts. It's the sacrifice in preferring the other's wishes over one's own. Yielding. Giving way. It's not easy, which is why we struggle. And when we struggle to make the equation work, conflict can arise.

Conflict does not have to be *expressed* to exist between the couple. It may be the silent partner in a marriage, standing in the shadows, reminding us of the other's shortcomings and the pain we have endured at the hands of the one we call *spouse*. Silence can be the enemy's greatest ally; it leaves the door open to whisper accusation in our ears, fortifying our outrage and pushing us further from resolution.

We can find ways to be candid and open in expressing our differences as we deal with conflict in a way that *develops* the relationship rather than *destroys* it. And only then will we begin to experience a new unity. The Word of God holds the keys to this process.

Christianity is not a psychological process; it's supernatural, a spiritual process in which our marriage is designed to exist. And while we will explore skills, tools, and approaches to equip us to deal with conflict effectively—building our understanding, our agreement, and ultimately our life together—we cannot do it apart from the reality that without His Spirit to guide us on the journey, we will fail.

There's no positive alternative to developing the spiritual understanding as well as the skills to resolve our differences. But many live with the negative outcome daily. Unresolved conflict leads to hurt, anger, pain, and dysfunction. This is true not only for the couple, but for their children, and as the stress becomes evident, for others in their extended circle of relationships. Unfortunately, Christ followers are not immune. In fact, in attempting to please God, we may stifle our conflict, pushing it down inside until it explodes onto center stage like an ugly jack-in-the-box.

Conflict is not the real problem. It's how we *deal* with the conflict that determines where it takes us. Conflict begins with a difference of opinion, experience, belief, or perception. It can lead to discovery—greater insight and understanding of our partner's thoughts, feelings, and perspective. But when it's handled poorly, carelessly, or callously, it can lead to damage and, ultimately, destruction of the relationship. It's up to us to choose which direction we will go—discovery or destruction.

We're proud of the forty years we've accumulated together, and we're just bright enough to know we didn't do it on our own. Without the willingness to let God's Word and His Spirit lead, we'd have blown it up long ago. The Lord never intended us to be self-sufficient, and we don't desire to be anything but dependent on Him. It's not always been easy, but it's always been worth the effort, made possible only by consistently renewing the commitment we made the day I wore the fancy dress and he wore the yellow tux (it seemed like a good idea at the time).

And while we will share pieces of our story, *Don't Go to Bed Angry* is not primarily about us. It's the compiled work of survey responses and conversations with couples who have generously shared their experiences with us—the good, the bad, and the tragic. In this book we combine those insights with our professional experience. I (Deb) have more than thirty years of teaching adults how to communicate, resolve conflict, and develop relationship. Ron has as many years of Christian counseling, instruction, and leadership development, primarily in ministry to men.

So if you're sick and tired of the futility of fighting the same battles the same way, leaving you exhausted and broken, we encourage you to hang up your gloves and walk away from that match. Let's explore the importance of healthy conflict and discover tools to fight together in a way that is aligned with scripture, honoring our union and our God. It *is* possible to develop a relationship of genuine understanding and intimacy, but it can occur only when Christ is our banner and love is our battle plan.

What's Ahead

As we began to examine conflict and its effect on marriage, a pattern emerged. This pattern is helpful in understanding the full impact of conflict, as well as the challenges, and opportunities, presented when a difference of opinion blossoms into potential conflict. It serves our recall as well, making key concepts stand out in our minds. Chapter 2 discusses the inevitability of conflict and its potential impact on the marriage relationship. Also, beginning with chapter 2, the book is organized by the six categories we discovered. They are:

1. Burdens (chapter 2)
2. Baggage (chapter 3)
3. Bridges (chapter 4)
4. Barriers (chapters 5, 6, 7)
5. Boundaries (chapter 8)
6. Blessings (chapter 9)

Let's take a look at them briefly.

BURDENS

When we pull back the curtain on conflict, we discover the damage it can inflict on the relationship between husband and wife.

Over time, unresolved conflict weighs a marriage down and destroys the heart of the union God intends us to experience. The day-to-day relationship becomes transactional and joyless. A marriage without intimacy is on its deathbed. It may remain there for many years, but no life or breath remains.

In chapter 2, we will discover the burden and impact of conflict, which underscores why it's essential to find a productive way to deal with it.

BAGGAGE

We all come to marriage with our stuff. Some of it is good stuff, and some of it is kind of stinky. Where did it come from? We weren't blank slates the day we stood at the altar. Our life experiences, our family norms, our past relationships, and even our education all contributed to the person we are the day we marry and the baggage we bring to the union. Those experiences leave an impression in our hearts and minds. They create expectations and patterns of thinking and behaving that can drive our spouses crazy. Some are inconsequential: *Mayo or Miracle Whip?* Some are significant: *Avoid discussing feelings at all costs. Just let it blow over. Tomorrow's another day.*

Just as there is a penalty for an overweight suitcase, that baggage is costing us. It's best to avoid the additional fee by leaving it behind. Chapter 3 will examine how to identify it and what to do about it.

BRIDGES

Once we leave the baggage behind (or at least know how to recognize it), we are ready to develop the skills required to make conflict a learning opportunity that creates alignment in the relationship and deters damage.

In chapter 4 we address both the willingness to address the

situation and the skill to do it well. That chapter introduces tools you can use to SPEAK up in the right way at the right time and the keys to stay calm. When conflict begins to get away from you, how can you bring it back to a constructive, rational conversation? It's possible if you have the right tools for the job.

BARRIERS

Even when both parties acknowledge the need to deal with conflict constructively and make a decision to "do better," we must address some barriers in order to succeed. Our past experiences with conflict resolution have taught us many lessons, few of which are useful in creating the discovery and agreement we seek.

Each of us has an individual response to conflict, a set of behaviors that constitute our style. In chapter 5, we examine conflict styles with a focus on creating a balanced playing field. From avoiding to competing, we will clarify the styles on the passive / assertive scale and learn how to become allies, not adversaries, fighting together for the life of the marriage.

There are communication approaches that can tear us apart when conflict arises. In chapter 6 we expose them for what they are—traps that lock us into an endless merry-go-round of disappointment. We'll shine a light on four of the most common communication traps.

There are multitudes of ways to deal with conflict that may not be harmful to the relationship between husband and wife but are damaging to us individually. Chapter 7 reinforces the reality that forgiveness is key. Without it, conflict can become an everyday occurrence as our ability to resurrect old wounds can become like the *Groundhog Day* movie where every day brings the same old stuff to the table. Our shared history is not always a gift; when there have been breaches in the level of trust, moving forward together is more complicated. "Forgive and forget" is not a concept most of us have experienced successfully. But we must address these two issues differently: forgiveness is a spiritual process and forgetting is a biological process. In "Your Past Doesn't Have to Be Your Future," we explore the concepts of love and law and discover ways to move from a contract-based relationship to a covenant relationship based on the love of Jesus and His Spirit.

BOUNDARIES

We've discarded the baggage, built some bridges, and identified major barriers. Our focus moving forward is to set aside negative patterns of behavior by replacing them with positive actions. We begin that work as we set up the conflict response parameters: identifying what's off-limits and out-of-bounds when conflict arises. The purpose is to ensure both parties are protected emotionally, spiritually, mentally, and physically.

In "Rules of Engagement: Learning to Fight Fair" (chapter 8) we review how to establish mutually agreeable boundaries that allow us to confront issues together without becoming confrontational with each other.

BLESSINGS

The focus in this final section is planning and preparing our lives together to result in the marriage God intended us to experience. Walking in agreement requires several steps: verifying vision, creating clarity, and achieving alignment in our lives.

Chapter 9, "How Do We Get There from Here," introduces a planning tool designed to spark conversation and ignite big dreaming, which achieves a unified vision for your marriage.

Put on the Gloves! Resource Sections

Boxing gloves are used in the ring to ensure that each individual is ready for the match, yet protected in the fight. Since you and your spouse will be learning to fight the forces that come against your marriage, we encourage you to *put on the gloves!* At the end of each chapter, you will find a section to prompt discussion about what you've read, along with ideas, principles, and insights that resonated with you. Each person should keep a journal to record his or her responses to the questions in this section. Recording your responses will help insure that you capture them while they're fresh. The section also includes support for continued conversation to grow and develop your relationship.

So let's get some experience and put on the gloves right now. It's a quick peek into what you can expect at the end of each section.

Put on the Gloves! Introduction

If possible, we recommend both spouses complete this entire section. Respond to the questions individually, and then come together for a discussion. If you are completing this process alone, record your thoughts to the questions and use the conversation starters for a discussion with your spouse. Record what each of you shares in the "He Said / She Said" section.

1. What's my primary reason for reading this book? What are my hopes and dreams for us as a couple?

2. On a scale of 1 to 10, with 1 rated as the lowest level of commitment and 10 as "I'm all in," how committed am I personally to completing the work to achieve those hopes and dreams, even if my spouse is not actively involved in this work?

3. What will it take to move to a higher level of commitment?

He Said / She Said

Use these questions to build a discussion with your spouse. Then each enter your thoughts in a "He Said / She Said" section of your journal.

- What hopes and dreams will we not realize until we can learn to resolve conflict that utilizes our differences in a way that develops rather than divides our relationship?
- How will this time be different? How can we approach this to support our success?

God Said

"We aren't fighting against human enemies but against rulers, authorities, forces of cosmic darkness, and spiritual powers of evil in the heavens." (Ephesians 6:12)

What does this mean to you? How does it change your

perception of conflict with your spouse? If it's spiritual warfare, how do you deal with it?

New Discoveries / How Can We Use This Information?

Be specific! Write in your journal what stands out to you from this chapter.

Prayer

We declare that you are the Lord of our lives, not just of us as individuals, but as a couple united in you. We believe the Scriptures are the key to successful marriage, and we surrender the lies of self-sufficiency. We acknowledge the Bible as the blueprint in the life of every Christian and believe that without it, we will never enjoy the experience marriage was intended to be. We recognize that you designed marriage as an example to the world of the love between you and your church, the bride of Christ. And we accept the responsibility to point a thirsty world to you through the relationship they see in our life together.

CHAPTER 1

WHAT'S WRONG WITH US? CAN'T WE JUST GET ALONG?

My daughter-in-law, Sarah, descended the stairs slowly. I glanced up from the sink, scraping a few breakfast remnants into the disposal. "Hi, sweets. How are you this morning?"

She turned in my direction, a look of concern on her fair face. "Uh…okay. How are *you?*" She slid onto the stool on the opposite side of the breakfast bar.

"I'm fine." My eyebrows shot up. "Why do you ask?"

She twisted a strand of her red hair. An old habit from her little girl days, I think. But whenever she did it, the message was clear: *I'm uncomfortable or anxious or something.* "You and Dad had a fight last night." She blurted the words onto the granite countertop, eyes not meeting mine.

"Oh. Yes. We did. Didn't realize you could hear us, honey. I'm sorry about that."

Her eyes searched mine. "But you *fight?* You guys seem so good together. I didn't think you ever did that."

I chuckled. "How do you think we've stayed married so long, Sarah? We're two strong personalities who've never struggled to express ourselves. It gets loud at times, but it's over pretty quick. My mom used to say it's not the vented pot that blows its stack. It's the one with the lid screwed on too tight that explodes. What you heard was us 'venting the pot.' At least no one around here will ever be able to say, 'Gee, I didn't know you felt that way.' "

Sarah's mother raised her on her own after Sarah's dad died. This sweet girl was only five at the time. She'd not been present for many dustups between married couples. It startled her. Later, she told me that hearing the fight between Ron and me made her feel better about the occasional arguments she and our son Jordan experienced. When I asked her why, her answer was simple: "Because it means you can disagree with someone you love and it doesn't have to ruin a relationship. It's bound to happen on occasion."

In other words, *I'm okay, you're okay*. Or maybe even, *Misery loves company*. Either way, Sarah was right.

Conflict Is Inevitable

Conflict is bound to happen. It *can* be healthy, a genuine asset to understanding each other. But it can also be harmful and dangerous. Whichever way it goes, one thing we do believe: conflict is inevitable. Two different individuals with different life experiences, even if both are committed Christ-followers, come to marriage with different approaches, ideas, preferences, and beliefs. And whether it ever becomes a verbal process or not isn't really the issue. Quiet in the house doesn't mean peace. Conflict originates—and sometimes lodges—in the heart.

Marriage is a continual work in progress; we never truly arrive at a place where we can say, "Well, then, that's it. We've got it nailed." As our lives change and shift with the years, so does our need for attention and commitment to making love last. We've met couples who have been married thirty years who are as mired in the difficulty of conflict as they were in year one. How can that be? They got stuck without a plan or path to grow in their relationship and as a result, they lack the *wisdom* of thirty years of experience. They have one year repeated thirty frustrating times.

Our primary goal for this book is to help you avoid that path. We believe you can build the required skill and knowledge to resolve life's conflict in a manner that honors the covenant of your marriage and deepens the relationship—not only between the two of you, but with God as well.

Beware the Real Enemy

The pretty redhead with the question at that conference where we spoke said to me privately as our evening concluded, "So it sounds like you *advocate* fighting. I'm not comfortable with that. It doesn't sound right to me."

I agreed with her; it's a concept that I had questions about over the years. I grew up in a home where, if my parents ever disagreed, it was never apparent to me. "Larry" was all my mother said on occasion to address my father's often-boisterous behavior. It came with a specific tone and a glance over the top of her glasses. And somehow for them, it did the trick. It was over. Right then. Unfortunately, I didn't inherit that gene. Or perhaps Ron simply ignores my gift. Either way, we usually require more than just one word.

Let us be clear: volume—whether in decibels or in the number of words—is not violence. But *behavior* that's out of control physically

3

or emotionally is out-of-bounds and should never be tolerated. It's not acceptable to God, and it shouldn't be acceptable to us as couples.

So is fighting the right approach? Is it even the correct term for what we do?

The title of this book may lead you to believe that we think stepping into the ring to take our shot at each other is a great resolution tactic. It's not. But fighting the *enemy*, together, for the life of our marriage *is*.

Remember that after the fall of the angels from the heavens, the first recorded act of the deceiver was to create division in the union between Adam and Eve and between them and God. (Genesis 3:1-11). It's our belief that if Satan can divide the marriage, he can divide the family. And if he can divide the family, he can divide the church.

God Holds Us Both Accountable

The church often finds itself in the center of marital conflict as couples seek counseling and support. Ephesians 4:26-27 is the source often quoted as part of the process: "And 'don't sin by letting anger control you.' Don't let the sun go down while you are still angry, for anger gives a foothold to the devil" (NLT). Every Christian couple on the planet has heard that particular message. It doesn't apply to marrieds alone, but it sure does seem to fit nicely.

My friend Marissa Star, married for more than fifteen years, took to Facebook to vent about this passage, perhaps one of the most misunderstood scriptures on the subject. I can't improve on what she said, so prepare for a rant.

> You know that scripture about not letting the sun go down on
> your anger, don't let the devil have a foothold? Yeah, that one. My

personal opinion after traumatizing my husband with my good Christian intentions the first two years of marriage is that this can be one of the most misunderstood or poorly taught marriage principles in the church. It leaves couples feeling like failures at 2 in the morning, exhausted as all get-out, trying to resolve issues that would be better talked through by two rested individuals who had time to reflect and gain some perspective.

The sun going down on your anger is about you dealing with your own anger, not keeping inventory of your spouse's anger or discussing how well he / she dealt with it. It takes five minutes with your eyes closed to give God your anger and get the devil off your foot, if you will. Let it go until a more beneficial time when you both have fresh perspective.

We couldn't agree more. The keys in this scripture are about personal responsibility: God holds each partner accountable for his or her behavior. The Bible is clear that it's possible to be angry without it becoming sinful. But to withhold forgiveness until the other party satisfies you, which may be unattainable in the moment, can be a problem. He expects us to forgive, even when the other party hasn't requested it. We believe it's God's love for us that calls us to let go of the ugliness, the hurt, or the pain, so we aren't damaged by it. Forgiving others benefits *us*, allowing us to move forward beyond the drama or the anger, on to the peace He quickly supplies. Making that choice is empowered and enabled by God's Spirit. We are not doing it in our strength, but by His.

I'm not going to pretend it's easy, and you may not *feel* like forgiving in the moment. But authentic love and successful marriage are not the results of feelings. Feelings are subject to change. Love and marriage are *choices*. Choose to forgive because it's the right thing to do and because it allows God's presence to infuse the remaining work that needs to be done. It's much easier to resolve the conflict and create a solution both can support if you are no longer adversaries, but allies, working together for the health of your relationship.

When our sons were growing up, the conflict often revolved around them and how to best raise them to be good humans and great men of God. We agreed on the *outcomes* we desired, but the opinions on the best *approach* sometimes varied widely. Other topics like spend versus save, and sex versus intimacy were often up for discussion. And don't forget the disagreements about who said he or she would do what, when, and now it's not done. Let's include the times we got embroiled in arguing about the argument and the tone of voice or the rolled eyes. After forty years together, the topics are different, but we still bump up against each other on occasion. *Is it just us?*

Discovering the answer to that question was our first step in the process of writing this book. We got nosy with friends and family, asking them about their conflicts. We read a lot of articles and did some research online. But eventually, we were interested in how people of faith dealt with this issue, and whether there were differences in approach when compared with those with no basis of faith at all. So we conducted some surveys and interviews of our own.

In chapter 3, we'll take some time to review what we discovered. But first, take a moment to complete *Put on the Gloves!*

Put on the Gloves! Chapter 1

If possible, we recommend both spouses complete this entire section. Respond to the questions individually, and then come together for a discussion. If you are completing this process alone, record your thoughts to the questions and use the conversation starters for a discussion with your spouse. Record what each of you shares in the "He said / She said" section.

1. What were three ideas, concepts, or elements in this chapter that stood out to you based on your experience with marital conflict? Why did they seem significant?

2. Complete this sentence: Our relationship would be so much stronger if we could just stop or start...

He Said / She Said

Use these questions to build a discussion with your spouse. Then each enter your thoughts in a "He Said / She Said" section of your journal.

- What do you believe about conflict?
- Is it inevitable?
- Are there any positive aspects to conflict? Could it be beneficial to our relationship? How?

God Said

"And 'don't sin by letting anger control you.' Don't let the sun go down while you are still angry, for anger gives a foothold to the devil" (Ephesians 4:26-27 NLT).

What new insight and understanding do you have regarding this scripture now?

New Discoveries / How Can We Use This Information?

Be specific! Write in your journal what stands out to you from this chapter.

Prayer

Father, we recognize that you created each of us as a unique human being, and while we may not always agree, we are yours and agree on your headship in our life together. Our hearts' desire for our marriage is to walk in the unity you envisioned for us, as we became one in marriage, knowing that it honors you and our covenant. We recognize that some of our behavior is an outpouring of your craftsmanship; other actions are born of our own desires, experiences, and preferences. Please help us accept each other as you made us to be and recognize where we need to become more like you, leaving the old behaviors behind. We ask you to help us as we move toward the reality that conflict can be an energizing and positive aspect of our relationship, leading to wholeness in our life together in you. We surrender the need to be right and submit to the goal of reflecting you in our relationship. We stand on the promise of your Word: "Again I assure you that if two of you agree on earth about anything you ask, then my Father who is in heaven will do it for you" (Matthew 18:19).

CHAPTER 2
IS IT JUST US?

Whether conflict grew unexpectedly out of a conversation that suddenly got away from us, or we stomped in and threw the doors open wide, the impact was almost always the same. The weight of the discord was tough all by itself, but at times the knowledge that we had let God down smothered us. The burden of conflict is the damage it leaves in its wake.

Does it have the same effect on all couples? Or do some have the ability to shake it off and go on unscathed? What creates conflict most often? And what are the secrets of those who manage it well? Those were among our top areas of interest in the research we conducted.

As we prepared our online surveys, we wanted to be clear about defining who our respondents would be. We asked them to identify whether they considered themselves persons of faith, along with gender, age, and other baseline questions. Nearly all of those in the first survey self-identified as Christ-followers. That was not a surprise. We sent the invitations for this survey to those in ministry, church groups, and those among our personal friends or acquaintances through Christian social media sites.

The second survey was open to all respondents through an online survey process. While many indicated they were Christians, the majority indicated no faith affiliation or a belief system. In total 235 men and women responded. The results were both surprising and enlightening.

The combined groups' marriage experience:

How long have you been married?

Less than two years	17 percent
2-5 years	23 percent
6-10 years	11 percent
11-20 years	35 percent
21-30 years	3 percent
31-40 years	10 percent
More than 40 years	1 percent

The great majority (80 percent) had been married once, with another 15 percent having made the trip to the altar twice. Just 4 percent had married three times with the ever hopeful 1 percent saying "I do" a total of five times.

The average length of their *current* marriage was in the 11–20 years range with the second largest group at 2–5 years.

What's All the Commotion About?

Since conflict was our topic, one of the most important questions was to discover the sources of the couples' conflicts. Here's what they told us (combined survey results):

Issue Ranked as #1 Cause of Conflict

Communication problems	33 percent
Feeling unappreciated by spouse	21 percent
Finances	20 percent
Childrearing issues	19 percent
Dissatisfaction/problems with sexual relationship	19 percent
Lack of affection	17.5 percent

The interesting and somewhat startling fact is that while the percentages shifted slightly between the two surveys, these categories were identical in their order of importance. The great majority of respondents indicated that conflicts attached to these issues happened on average of three times per month.

Nearly 50 percent believed that *conflict is inevitable* in marriage. Although many acknowledged that conflict could be damaging (25 percent), a larger percentage indicated it could be *helpful to the expression of thoughts and feelings* (60 percent) and a healthy way to gain insight and understanding (49 percent), and 59 percent believed that done well, *conflict could help spouses grow together.* That was encouraging news.

One set of responses we found particularly amusing (and very familiar to us personally) was that in the majority of cases, respondents saw themselves as far more skilled than their spouses when it came to using effective conflict resolution tactics. Why is that funny? Because it's common to judge ourselves on our intentions rather than solely on our actions. This allows us to assign ourselves extra credit even if the behaviors were a little wonky. On the other hand, my mate? *Oh, don't even get me started!* (Don't look so innocent; you've done it too! It's human.)

The tools described by respondents as effective included empathy, communication, listening, and anger management skills. Just one out of every three found his or her spouse equally skilled, and only one out of six scored his or her spouse as more highly skilled than him- or herself. It would be interesting to see if their mates agreed with that assessment!

In addition to the statistical data, here are just a few of the anecdotal comments:

- "We had no conflict. I didn't know we had any issues since we never argued until he left me for another woman after eleven years of marriage."
- "We tend to ignore issues rather than talk them out."
- "My husband is known in his family as the *get-along guy*. He has such a 'mercy motivational' gift that sometimes it gets in the way of resolving the conflict between us."
- "My spouse refuses to communicate or resolve any issues. All he says is, 'It's okay.' But it's *not.*"

The impact of the conflict was also vividly described.

"I knew our eighteen-year marriage had hit a rough patch, but I was stunned to return home after a conference (which he encouraged me to attend) to an empty apartment. His rationale: *I just don't love you anymore.* Apparently there were issues I was not aware of and he was unwilling to seek counseling to address them once he shared them with me."

The heartache, loss, and disappointment experienced by both husbands and wives, the children, and the extended family were painful and penetrating. Even in cases when the marriage continued, despair was often consistently fed—kept current and alive—through anger or withdrawal, creating a vicious cycle of hopelessness and pain: "She shuts down, withdraws, and pretends there's no problem. Eventually, I just stopped trying. Our youngest has three more years until graduation. I've got to hold on until then. After that, well I'm just not sure I can do it anymore."

Impact: Damage or Discovery?

The most worrisome statistic was the response to the following question: "Have you experienced conflict in your marriage that you would classify as damaging or destructive?" Of those surveyed, 72 percent answered yes. When given the opportunity to elaborate on the information, responses included:

- "We continually wounded one another with our words."
- "I don't feel heard or listened to."
- "We are feast or famine. The volcano erupts, the pressure is relieved, and then it quietly builds up again."
- "Lots of selfishness on both sides. It killed my first marriage."

Also disturbing was the number (42 percent) of those who identified as people of faith but reported they *seldom or never* used their beliefs in resolving marriage conflict. How can it be that our faith gives us so little advantage? What happens to us during conflict that causes our Christian principles not to provide us with a foundation when tempers flare?

Very few reported what we would consider extreme or dangerous behavior—at least in their current relationships. But in some cases, there were reports of conflict involving verbal and emotional abuse: "My spouse will use force to get his way. I am bullied, threatened and subjected to his temper until he gains the solution he prefers."

If conflict is not addressed successfully, disappointment and discouragement weigh down the relationship. Despair and damage attempt to pile on. The burden of conflict can suck the joy out of what started with such hope.

Encouraging News

But it's not all grim. When we asked, "If you are satisfied with the approach you manage conflict as a couple, what are you doing right?" here's what they told us:

- "Our success comes from talking it out, gaining perspective, and adjusting our expectations."
- "We've worked very hard at this. Showing respect, communicating clearly, focusing on whatever is praiseworthy and having fun together."
- "We learned how each other is wired, and applied the tools we have discovered. It's a matter of finding your own rhythm."

- "We are committed to following a process we learned early in our marriage. It works because it created shared tools and common language that moves us into productive territory fairly quickly."

What pattern do you spot in the two contrasting sets of comments? Communication is essential, as is the willingness to work together—to fight *together*, if you will, for your marriage. And most important, these skills weren't automatically built-in when they said, "I do."

The Right Tools Bring Right Results

Did we find our answer? Yes. It's *not* just us. *And it's not just you either.* We've been married for many years. Much of what we learned took us longer than we wish it had. We don't have all the answers or a perfect record in using what we know. What we have acquired through our life experience and through God's Word is the understanding that marriage is worth fighting for, and you don't have to be born knowing how to do it. If this has been an area of struggle or shame, or if you've believed the lie that you two are simply big failures, stop beating yourself up.

Anything worth building requires an investment in the right tools. Most of us are a bit on the light side in the tool department when we marry. We come with starry eyes and a heartfelt commitment based on what we know about marriage *in that moment.* The vast majority of us didn't have a clue what it meant to say "I do."

We don't know how to *do* marriage until we're in the mix, but it doesn't keep us from having lots of opinions about how it *should* be done. Remember thinking how your love was different from other people's you'd known? How it would last a lifetime, and that on the strength of your incredible feelings for each other, "happily ever after" was your certain destiny? Then reality hit. It's kind of like the difference between reading about the rodeo and strapping yourself to a bucking bronco. It's filled with surprises and can become a wild ride right out of the gate.

I've come to believe that surprises are only good at your birthday, and a wild ride is just fine as long as I've signed up for the adventure. Remembering to pack light helps to make the journey enjoyable and safe for all involved. The baggage we drag along with us may need to be tossed if we are to arrive without the penalty of heaviness it levies.

In the next chapter we'll examine how that baggage attached itself to us in the first place. But for now, take a moment to reflect on the insights from this chapter by completing the *Put on the Gloves!* resource section.

Put on the Gloves! Chapter 2

If possible, we recommend both spouses complete this entire section. Respond to the questions individually, and then come together for a discussion. If you are completing this process alone, record your thoughts to the questions and use the conversation starters for a discussion with your spouse. Record what each of you shares in the "He said / She said" section.

1. What statistics or comments from our survey respondents had an impact on you? Why did they seem significant? Which were familiar? Which ones did you relate to most?

2. What role does your faith play in how you deal with conflict? On a scale of 1 (least often) to 10 (most often), how frequently do you turn to biblical principles, prayer, or Scripture for direction? How do you feel about that number?

He Said / She Said

Use these questions to build a discussion with your spouse. Then each enter your thoughts in a "He Said / She Said" section of your journal.

- How transparent are we about the impact conflict has on us? our family? others?
- Let's get honest: how effective are we in dealing with conflict so it's not damaging?
- What steps can we take to make our faith more present in the way we deal with conflict?

God Said

"But in all these things we win a sweeping victory through the one who loved us" (Romans 8:37).

Knowing the challenges that come against marriage, realizing you are not alone in this fight, what does this Scripture represent for your experience as husband and wife?

New Discoveries / How Can We Use This Information?

Be specific! Write in your journal what stands out to you from this chapter.

Prayer

Father, it's clear that you are grieved by the behavior that conflict can incite, because you love us and want what's best for us. Jesus already bore the full weight of our sin, and we declare that when conflict arises we will not welcome it back into our lives. We will resist the enemy's temptation to use our differences to divide us and distract us from our desire to finish this race, together, in you. We invite you to infuse our hearts and minds, to direct us through your Spirit, and to remind us of the sacrifice of your son, Jesus, when we are tempted to let anger, conflict, or hurt direct our conduct when differences arise. We submit to your Word:

"Since we are surrounded by so great a cloud of witnesses, let us lay aside every weight, and the sin which so easily ensnares us, and let us run with endurance the race that is set before us" (Hebrews 12:1 NKJV).

CHAPTER 3

Leave that Baggage on the Carousel!

"I just can't deal with the emotion anymore. I'm a *practical* person. I'm *rational*, and my spouse wants to tell me all about how he *feels*. Can't we just leave the emotional baggage out of it and have an adult conversation?"

The short answer is no.

The ever-logical Mr. Spock of *Star Trek* fame may have made the galaxy a safer place, but did he ever fall in love? Was he married? No! Did he ever look as though he was having a good time? Not that we can recall. We can't simply sever our emotions from our interactions and relationships, and more importantly, we shouldn't try.

We are created in the image of our God. And when He created us, He did so with a capacity for emotion. It's one of the ways we reflect the Lord to those around us: "This is how everyone will know that you are my disciples, when you love each other" (John 13:35).

God has emotions and feels them deeply. How do we know? "God *so* loved the world, that he gave his only Son" (John 3:16). God loves and feels joy, sorrow, and wrath. Jesus' life here on earth included frustration, love, and disappointment, to name a few strong emotions. And the Holy Spirit is the comforter. God fashioned us as God is.

The idea of leaving the emotions out of a conflict or conversation may sound good on the surface, but are you interested in discussing differences with your loved one without mercy, grace, patience, and forgiveness attending? And would you surrender the positive emotions when joy and unity are restored?

So it's safe to say, God created us with the capacity for emotional needs and responses. But I do understand the frustration of those who'd like to set emotion aside in favor of a practical and logical approach. God expects us to manage our emotions and not let them manage us.

Managing the Emotional Roller Coaster

Just as difficult as those with out-of-control emotions are those who deny their emotions altogether, keeping their feelings tightly under wraps. They may be the scariest of the lot. We never know what might be brewing beneath those brows. This approach denies our humanity, deprives our partners of empathy, and makes intimacy impossible. Both of these extremes are unhealthy and out of alignment with who God created us to be.

But life is a roller coaster if emotions are allowed to *rule* our behavior. A constant tumbling between one extreme and the other wears out the people in our lives. The lack of balance is exhausting. Think about King David as revealed in the Psalms. The man after God's "own heart" (Acts 13:22 NIV) never did or felt anything halfway. When he was happy, he was ecstatic. When he was sad, he was certain life was over. And when he was led by his feelings, they took him where God grieved to see him go. Yet God specifically chose David.

God longs to see us individually and as a couple move to maturity, both spiritually and emotionally. How do we do that? First, accept that spiritual maturity is impossible without emotional health. Second, acknowledge that emotional health develops when we submit our feelings to the Lord and His Word.

For a couple to be emotionally healthy, each partner has to find emotional balance and wellness. When we are able to manage our own emotions and develop the ability to respond appropriately to others' emotions, we have a new set of possibilities open to us as marrieds.

How did we not learn to do this before we marry? Where are the vulnerability classes or the Empathy 101 courses? Some of us learned it early in life through role models such as parents, friends, teachers, pastors, or school counselors. But many of us either weren't paying attention, or those shining examples of emotional well-being failed to show up in our lives. Many of us make our way to the altar without a solid understanding of the importance of the baggage we may drag along for the ride.

Let's explore this a bit more by introducing Rick and Roxanne.

Let's Meet Rick and Roxanne

Rick and Roxanne have been married four years. They met during Rick's final year in college, when Roxanne was a freshman.

Her flat tire during an afternoon rainstorm near the library parking lot caught Rick's attention as he ran to his car. He encouraged her to take refuge in the library while he fixed her flat. Although she was a bit uncomfortable handing her keys to a stranger, Roxanne gratefully accepted his help. When he found her inside thirty minutes later to return her keys, he asked for her number and their courtship began.

Their relationship developed quickly and four months later, the night of his graduation, Rick proposed. Roxanne was surprised and concerned when she learned he had already accepted a job in a nearby state, but he promised her that the new position would mean she'd be able to finish college as his wife. Roxanne was thrilled and quickly accepted. A small wedding six weeks later with family and close friends celebrated their new life together.

Roxanne enjoyed her new role and took pride in keeping her home and her homework in excellent condition. Rick followed his dad's lead and put in great effort to do well in his new job. He also remembered Uncle Bob's advice to step up as the spiritual head of his home and selected a church near their apartment for weekly services.

Rick was promoted quickly and within fourteen months he was offered a new position on the other side of the country. His announcement that they'd be moving caught Roxanne off-guard. Her studies were going well and she'd been accepted into an important intern program for the following school year. Rick reassured her she had adjusted well to the initial move and he was confident she would have no problem doing it again. Roxanne was disappointed not to finish her program and resented that she hadn't even been consulted before Rick made his decision.

Additionally, he had committed to the move within the next six weeks. The timing meant she would be unable to finish the current semester. She'd have to withdraw and repeat the courses in their new location. But Roxanne was very proud of Rick and decided to celebrate their great fortune with a rare dinner out together rather than to spoil his news with her complaining.

When Rick appeared the following night with a brand-new car, she was stunned. It was a beauty. She sat in the luxurious interior and quickly discovered it was a manual shift vehicle, which she'd never learned to drive. And she was upset by Rick's response when she'd asked the price of the car. "Don't you worry about it, baby. We can afford it." Once again, she'd been excluded from what she thought was an important family decision.

The pattern continued over the next eighteen months, with another move related to Rick's work delaying her graduation once again. Roxanne fielded a few calls from their bank asking when the car payment would be received and one about the status of some credit cards she'd not been aware of. When she mentioned the calls to Rick, he abruptly told her it wasn't her concern and that he'd take care of it. Roxanne wanted to discuss it, but he put his arms around her and told her not to worry, that it was a mistake and he'd be sure to clear it up. She dropped it and the phone calls ended.

And now, nearly four years later, Roxanne is finally anticipating graduation in just two weeks and preparing for her transition to a new career. But today's mail brought an unhappy surprise. She received a note from the university regarding the issue of her unpaid tuition for the final semester. The letter informed her that the university would be unable to finalize her grades and process her diploma until the final bill was paid. She could walk in the ceremony if she'd like, but until the tuition was settled, there would be no degree granted.

She's shocked, angry, and in disbelief. This time she won't let Rick put her off. He'll have to explain what's going on. It makes her physically ill to think about what might happen, but she knows she can't accept his false reassurances any longer.

How did they get here?

As we'll learn about Rick and Roxanne, our early life shapes us and either helps us or holds us back in developing emotional wellness before we say, "I do." We'll circle back for the rest of their story, but first let's step back and gain insight into the process that contributes to who we become.

What Makes Us Who We Are?

It begins with our experiences in life—they are imprinted on us, on our hearts and minds. They are real to us. We were there. No one can talk us out of our experiences. Our experiences create in us a set of beliefs. Those beliefs direct the actions we take, and the actions we take in life ultimately define the world in which we live.

Many relationships, including those with our parents, our siblings, and our extended family, contribute to the way we're shaped. Other factors involve where we were raised, churched, schooled, and even our neighborhood experiences. Were our families expressive and close or disconnected and detached? Did others generally accept us or were we bullied? Were we confident to join in activities or did we watch from the sidelines? The list goes on and on. All of these past experiences helped shape who we became. And when we married, we brought our own sets of experiences, beliefs, actions, and perspectives with us.

But what about Jesus? Where does He figure in? Good question—hang on to that. Let's look first at Rick and Roxanne and unpack their challenges with regard to conflict. Roxanne's story first.

EXPERIENCE

Growing up, Roxanne witnessed her mother's withdrawal when her dad became upset. Her mom, Evelyn, remained quiet and simply endured the verbal abuse her husband dished out, never defending herself or attempting to share her own thoughts. Although it frightened Roxanne and she feared her parents might divorce, Evelyn reassured her by saying things like, "Well, you know your dad is kind of excitable. I know how much he loves me. He didn't mean anything by that." Roanne's dad usually slammed out of the house after a big fight but often returned with flowers or a gift and an apology. Big hugs and smiles all around. The couple was married fifty-seven years when her father died. Evelyn had never seemed unhappy, and Roxanne was grateful to have lived in a home where her parents were committed to their marriage.

BELIEFS

Roxanne believed her parents' approach to remaining married was successful. After all, a marriage that lasted more than five decades was proof. Growing up, although Roxanne was more outspoken by nature, she learned it often attracted negative attention from her dad. Her mother pointed out the best way to avoid unpleasantness was never to engage in the discord. When Roxanne became engaged to Rick, she accepted her mother's counsel to remain silent during marital disagreements and to "simply let it blow over" as good advice.

ACTIONS

Roxanne lives her mother's life. Her actions mirror those she learned as a young girl. Although Rick does not bully her, Roxanne is convinced that is because she refrains from arguing with him when she silently disagrees. They've been married four years and have really never had what she would call a "fight."

WORLD

As a result, she is often dissatisfied about the decisions he makes about their finances and resents that he makes decisions without including her in the discussion. Her schooling has been impacted on several occasions, and she now lives in fear for their financial situation even though she is unaware of the details except one: she will not receive her degree as expected.

How about Rick? Let's take a look.

EXPERIENCE

Rick's parents were high school sweethearts who married right after graduation. His dad, Raymond, built a successful home construction business from the ground up, while his mother was a full-time homemaker and stay-at-home mom. If there was ever any discord between them, Rick was not aware of it, and he always felt as though they were very well matched. His mother managed the finances at home and also did the books for the business as her way of helping out. When the construction business fell on hard times, his father was caught by surprise and worked hard to save it. But the business eventually failed. Soon after, the family home was lost and they moved in with Rick's grandparents. And although his parents had brought Rick up in church, his parents divorced within a year and his father has not been present in his life since.

BELIEFS

Rick believed his dad had relied on his mother too much and did not stay well informed about important financial matters, and that fact eventually caused the business and the family to fail. Rick believed that he had to take full and complete responsibility for his life, without involving or relying on anyone's support or input.

ACTIONS

"The details matter" became Rick's motto and he was fastidious about every personal and financial decision he made. He worked two jobs to put himself through school and felt proud to complete his education without any debt or anyone's help in the process. When he married, he believed his life and his family were his responsibility alone. Since the responsibility was his, he did not feel it necessary to involve Roxanne in decisions that he felt he was better qualified to make.

WORLD

As a result, Rick has always been the decision-maker and breadwinner. His job is currently at risk, as his company has downsized and salary reductions have been implemented. Rick's performance is lower than others in his group, as he had far less experience when he accepted this new role than most of those in the job. He opened two credit card accounts to help tide over his family with household expenses and both are maxed out. He has not shared any of this information with Roxanne because he doesn't want to worry her. After all, there's nothing she could do. He's missed the last two car payments and did not pay her final tuition payment; he'd hoped his spring bonus would be sufficient to cover it. It wasn't. How on earth would he manage this? He realizes this time he can't fix it and will have to come clean with Roxanne about their situation.

Rick and Roxanne's Opportunity

Rick doesn't know it yet, but when he walks in the front door, he will face a difficult conversation. Is there hope for a positive outcome for this couple? Yes! For the first time ever, Rick and Roxanne will be creating a brand-new experience as they are forced to discuss their situation. And when we have new experiences, we open up the potential for new and different outcomes. Will it be easy? No. Uncomfortable? Probably. And if they can be open with each other, they are about to learn an important lesson: their combined baggage may match, but it's weighing them down.

They learned what they lived and are now trying to live those lessons out in their life together. Whose experience was better, Rick's or Roxanne's? Neither was great, but that's not the point. There are two important truths here: Their experiences were *real*. And their experiences were *different*. They could argue all day about which one is the better approach, but they will make progress together only if they recognize the *best* approach is the one they create together, with the Lord as their champion.

Making our way to emotional health requires us to discard the stuff from our pasts that doesn't build the life we desire together in Christ and embrace the new lessons God's Spirit and His Word will draw out of us. The important message here is that emotional fitness is not a birthright; it's something we can learn and for the Christ follower, the Word of God and the Holy Spirit are the best teachers available.

Why bother? The answer is that close, intimate relationships are impossible without emotional health.

Emotional Health Is Key

You and your spouse may be of the same faith, share common values, goals, interests, and activities. You may find pleasure in each other's company and experience strong chemistry or sexual attraction. But if emotions are ignored or minimized, the relationship will never move beyond a superficial level. When the relationship is shallow, conflict is difficult to resolve because we lack the intimacy that motivates us to build a solution.

When we *do* connect with our mates on an emotional level, it's surprising how quickly the relationships, even when quite new, become deep and personal. Think about those fast friendships that developed at retreats or summer camp when you were a kid, when the ability to be transparent with others created the tearful good-bye at the end of the week. Ron and I spent our first date talking for eight hours nonstop about our hopes and dreams, interests and fears. Ron told me later that he was drawn to me because I was interested in what he thought, felt, and had to say. It was unusual for him to discuss such topics and he was surprised by my curiosity. Vulnerability breeds strong, intimate ties. And when conflict arises for those with strong ties, spouses feel an authentic desire to find resolution quickly and restore full agreement. The couple is highly motivated to find a solution both can support.

We will always feel some level of isolation or aloneness without connecting on an emotional level. Married couples sometimes exist more like roommates than lovers. They share the expenses, split up the chores, and politely inform the other of plans that might require a missed dinner or night away. But there's no depth. Loneliness stalks the relationship.

A new acquaintance disclosed recently, "My spouse and I are both driven. We push ourselves to build career opportunity, regardless of the cost. We're both on a fast track for promotion and there's no real connection in our marriage. But it's okay, because we never see each other anyway." Later I asked about the couple's teenage daughters and the impact of the marriage relationship on them. "Well, yeah, there's that, I guess," he responded. And sadly, he has no idea of the widespread effect it will have not only on his girls, but on their spouses, and perhaps even on generations yet to come.

Our Baggage

Ron and I came to our wedding with a very mismatched set of baggage. Some had been passed down from parents and even grandparents. There were some lessons and patterns we'd learned in our respective experiences that were valuable. We could agree they'd be helpful as we built our life together so we added them to our repertoire. Others were the source of pain and brokenness; we had witnessed the dysfunction they bred. Those we left on the luggage carousel and walked away.

The successful process evolved over time. We didn't sit down in the middle of wedding planning one afternoon and take inventory. Some behaviors were obvious to us from the beginning. Others surfaced in the middle of a conversation or a conflict arose as our experiences clashed. Often the only thing we knew to do in those moments was pray.

Turns out, prayer was far better than anything we could have come up with on our own. God was, and always is, faithful when we come for comfort, for direction, and for forgiveness when it's gotten out of hand. "But anyone who needs wisdom should ask God, whose very nature is to give to everyone without a second thought, without keeping score. Wisdom will certainly be given to those who ask" (James 1:5).

So how do we leave that baggage on the carousel and free

ourselves from the extra weight it imposes? Like Rick and Roxanne, you will have to face your giants in authentic conversation. You may need outside help if the issues have driven a stake through the center of your emotional connection. Or you may be in the place where all you need are some new tools to get started. And that will be our focus in our next chapter.

For now, are you ready to put on the gloves and dump that baggage once and for all? Let's do it.

PUT ON THE GLOVES! CHAPTER 3

If possible, both spouses should complete this entire section. Respond to the questions individually, and then come together for a discussion. If you are completing this process alone, record your thoughts to the questions and use the conversation starters for a discussion with your spouse. Record what each of you shares in the "He said / She said" section.

1. What emotional baggage have you brought into your marriage that is holding you back from a healthy approach to deal effectively with conflict? What's the impact on your relationship?

2. What emotional baggage is your spouse bringing to the marriage? Identify one specific example that illustrates this. What's the impact on the level of connection and intimacy you share?

HE SAID / SHE SAID

Use these questions to build a discussion with your spouse. Then each enter your thoughts in a "He Said / She Said" section of your journal.

- How satisfied are you with the level of emotional connection we share?
- What are the casualties of the current level of emotional intimacy? Who or what is impacted?
- What kind of help do we need to improve our level of emotional health?

GOD SAID

"But anyone who needs wisdom should ask God, whose very nature is to give to everyone without a second thought, without keeping score. Wisdom will certainly be given to those who ask" (James 1:5).

When you consider this Scripture, how does it apply to your baggage? Does your past have to be part of your life today if it does not serve God or your marriage?

New Discoveries / How Can We Use This Information?

Be specific! Write in your journal what stands out to you from this chapter.

Prayer

Dear Lord, we thank you for the lessons of experience. The good ones show us what to repeat, and the bad ones tell us which ones to discard. Help us as we sort through those experiences we've brought into our relationship and direct us according to the scriptures by your Holy Spirit. We desire the intimate connection you envision for us as husband and wife and ask you for the wisdom we need to pursue it with our whole hearts. Heal the hurt caused by hauling around the baggage we needed to leave behind. We ask for the strength and understanding to push past old behavior. We submit to your Word: "Get wisdom! Get understanding before anything else" (Proverbs 4:7). "The beginning of wisdom is the fear of the Lord; the knowledge of the holy one is understanding" (Proverbs 9:10).

CHAPTER 4

Communication Tools That Work

Can we talk? That question has dual facets: Are we *willing* to discuss our differences in a transparent and open manner, and are we *skilled* and capable of doing so?

Even if both parties can wholeheartedly say Yes! to the first question, without the affirmative answer for question two, the result of the interaction will be frustration and disappointment. A steady diet of those two emotions will create hopelessness, even for the most motivated couples.

When we circle back to the topics that create the greatest number of conflicts, we begin to see some connections. Let's review them.

Issue Ranked as #1 Cause of Conflict	
Communication problems	33 percent
Feeling unappreciated by spouse	21 percent

Finances	20 percent
Child-rearing issues	19 percent
Dissatisfaction / problems with sexual relationship	19 percent
Lack of affection	17.5 percent

Communication is number one on the list. How do you deal with the rest of the items on the list if you are unable to communicate effectively?

My attempt to make my husband aware that I'm feeling unappreciated may not come across as a request for acknowledgment. It may sound like whining because he didn't notice I picked up his dry cleaning on my way home from work. And if he's already feeling as though I'm not making our sexual relationship a priority and things have gotten a little sparse in the affection department, then my request to be appreciated may get on his last nerve.

Communication skills are foundational to life. Couples who do this well have a huge advantage. Those who struggle often find themselves wondering, *Why doesn't my significant other get it? What's so difficult about this?*

Our survey respondents had a lot to say about this:

- "He's not stupid. He understands every word I'm saying. But he doesn't listen and when he does, he pretends like he doesn't know what I'm talking about. It's maddening."
- "My spouse is too emotional and ceases to be rational. It bugs the heck out of me, and when it happens, I'm done."
- "When conflict arises I don't feel heard or taken seriously."
- "We communicate differently, we don't express ourselves in

the same way. More often than not we discover we are actually saying the same thing. But we have to work through a lot of frustration to *hear* one another."

Not surprisingly, couples who are highly satisfied with their ability to deal with conflict in a productive way cite communication skills as their top-secret weapon to achieving agreement. From the survey:

- "Most of the time, as we talk it through, remembering to be respectful and not interrupt one another, it's productive. It opens the doors for understanding one another better."
- "Talking it out, gaining perspective is exhausting, but worth it. Would like to be able to get there without it costing us so much time and emotion."
- "It's a relief to be able to disclose the truth of how I feel when something is wrong and there is division between us."
- "We work at listening to one another; we've learned we must talk things out. The key for us is communication and openness with one another."

So as these couples have experienced, it *is* possible to achieve a level of communication that unites us, even in the midst of our differences. The other common thread here is that doing this well requires determined effort. It can feel like pushing a stone uphill, and for many of us, it may never become completely intuitive.

Communication Is More Than Just Talking

Communication is tricky business. Talking is easy, but authentic communication is not. So what is communication? A reliable and common definition is: *the transmission of a message so that both parties have a shared understanding of what's been said.* In other words, we assign the same meaning to the words spoken. Think about the times you've ended a discussion with your spouse and both felt very clear about the message, only to discover you had very different interpretations about what had been said. "That's what you *said*" is met with "But that's not what I *meant*—and you know it!" And so the drama begins, made more difficult with an accusation tossed in for fun.

Other contributing factors can short-circuit our conversation. As we learned in the previous chapter, our experiences shape how we see *and hear* things. We will address trust issues in a future chapter, but it, too, figures in. If trust is broken or in question, we begin listening between the lines for things unsaid, attaching meaning to every tilt of the head, tone of voice, and twitch of the brow. The result of this type of interpretation often sounds something like, "Well, I know you *said* you'd take care of the kids while I went out with the girls, but it was *clear* you wanted to go to the game with your brother!" The assumption is made and motive is assigned and conflict begins to brew.

For many, conflict is so uncomfortable that they decide to forego the conversation entirely in order to keep the peace. Don't ever mistake quiet in the house for agreement in the heart. *Silence is not peace.* It's avoidance and it's one of the most cavernous and damaging places to find yourself, as we will discover in chapter 6. Even if a couple has cut off all communication on a topic, the conflict is alive and well. It's just unspoken. They may talk about it—just not to each other. We look for allies who will share our outrage, and we feel better when others jump on our "I can't believe he did that to you!" bandwagon. We feel vindicated—at least *someone* agrees with us.

And validation moves us further from resolving the conflict because we have the satisfaction that others know *I was right.*

Many of us lack confidence, knowledge, or instruction on communicating effectively, so we sit on our feelings, letting our thoughts and concerns go unexpressed. Unexpressed, that is, until we can no longer maintain the silence and blow up, often in dramatic and unproductive ways. We've just created a greater problem, as words expressed in anger are often ugly and damaging. Mom's advice, "If you can't say anything nice, then don't say anything at all," is not practical for most of us, especially with our mates. "I was just speaking the truth in love," I recall saying to Ron after a particularly bitter exchange. It couldn't have been further from the truth and we both knew it, but it's become the all-purpose whitewash for Christian couples who are looking for an excuse to take off the gloves and bare-knuckle it.

Learning to SPEAK Up

So how do you open the lines of communication? How do you establish good communication, helping you avoid conflict more easily and deal with it more constructively when it occurs? If the relationship is not in turmoil but is less transparent, candid, and kind than you'd like it to be, building solid communication skills is a smart investment. As with anything you'd like to build, you need some tools. Let's learn to SPEAK the truth authentically in love. And God will happily lend you some of His love if you find it tough to produce on your own.

SPEAK is an easy acronym to help us remember that communication requires skill to create a peaceful process with a peaceable result. Here are the five components of SPEAK.

S—seek permission to have the discussion.

P—present the issue, concern, or idea.

E—explore solutions / ask questions.

A—acknowledge what you hear.

K—keep focused on the present, not past history.

Let's take a look at each of these components.

SEEK PERMISSION TO HAVE THE DISCUSSION

Have you ever walked in the door after work, juggling your briefcase, the groceries you stopped to pick up, and the mail tucked under one arm, only to find your husband or wife waiting to engage you the minute you set foot in the door with an important discussion that just won't wait? *Not now!* our brains scream. It's just not the right time. We're not in the best frame of mind for discussing anything more important than finding a comfortable place to collapse and catch our breath.

Timing, as they say, is everything. It's an important component of successful communication. If you have the right message at the wrong time, you will often be disappointed with the result. You never know what the other person's day has been like or whether he or she is struggling with something that makes this a bad time for a conversation. I (Deb) have a wonderful friend who always says when I pick up the phone, "Hi. I wanted to talk with you about our weekend plans. Is this a good time?" In other words, *she seeks permission* before launching ahead, allowing me to commit to the conversation or suggest an alternate time. It's respectful of my life, my time, and my mind-set in the moment. And it sets the stage for successful communication.

We'd never barge into the office of our boss or a colleague and launch into a lengthy discussion without first checking to see if he or she has a moment to spend with us. Yet with family, and particularly with our spouses, we assume, *If I need to talk to you about something right this minute, it's a good time for you too.* Dangerous assumption.

This is especially true in the digital world we live in today. E-mail, text, and phones are all convenient methods of staying in touch. But when we use them, we are blind to what's happening in the life of the person on the other end. We simply pick up that device and start "talking." I've received texts in the middle of dinner, and if no immediate response is given, I get a "HELLO???" I've also been guilty of doing it myself more often than I care to admit. We've come to believe we're *entitled* to communicate with another person at any time *we* choose—as though it's our right. But it's not.

When we seek permission, we are demonstrating respect for the other person. It gives him or her a voice to help define whether this moment is optimum for a positive outcome. Seeking permission helps us start off with mutual readiness.

If an earlier argument simply ended when one of you withdrew, or if a time of silence was extended over an upset, be specific when you seek permission. "I'd like to talk with you about our plans for the camping trip this summer. Last night we were both tired and the conversation went south on us. Would this be a good time for us to talk about it?" Readiness equals opportunity for success. Without it, the conversation may be doomed before it gets started.

What if the answer is "Not now"? Good to know—and the next question then is "When would be a better time for us to talk?"

Let's take a look at how this might go for Rick and Roxanne. She's waiting for him, and the conversation is going to be challenging. She will have to manage her emotions in order to have any real chance at making this work. She's nervous; she's not experienced with conversations like this and the voice of her mother floats overhead reminding her to avoid conflict. But she knows she can't ignore it.

"Rick, I want to talk with you about the letter I received from the university today regarding my unpaid tuition. The letter states my diploma will be held until the fees are paid in full. I was surprised to learn there was a problem since you have managed our finances by yourself. We need to discuss the situation and come up with a plan since graduation is only a few weeks away. Would you be open to doing that now?"

Please note that the question Roxanne asks is closed-ended; it requires only a yes or no response from Rick. It brings him to a decision point: *Will you discuss this with me now?*

PRESENT INFORMATION

Once both of you have committed to the conversation, the next step is to *present information*. Examples include:

- Sharing information, ideas, or thoughts on the topic you want to discuss.
- Identifying a concern you want to address and explaining why it's a concern for you.
- Disclosing an opinion or perspective on an issue, opportunity, or event.

This is your chance to begin the conversation by clearly explaining what you think or feel and why it warrants discussion.

Have you ever found yourself wondering ten minutes into a conversation, *What's she rambling about? I can't even follow the train of thought. If she has a point, I wish she'd just get to it.* We wear people out when we fail to organize and express our thoughts effectively so they can participate in the conversation in a meaningful way. Sometimes it's uncomfortable to get down to business, so we try to *work up* to it or *back into it.* Don't.

Be straightforward and clear in the information you present. Don't beat around the bush, as it requires others to fill in the gaps with their own assumptions. Assumptions create a shaky foundation when it comes to building good communication.

So, it might sound something like this: "Rick, for the four years we've been married you've always been in charge of our finances. You pay the bills, do the banking, and arranged the car loan. Initially, it was nice to be taken care of. You were willing to shoulder all the responsibility and I felt protected, safe. It let me focus on school and not have to worry about the bills.

"But on the few occasions I asked questions about our financial situation, like the price of the car and whether we could really afford it, you dismissed me without a response. It made me feel like a kid, living at home with my folks. And then when the bank called about a missed car payment and credit cards I didn't know we had, I was upset. When I tried to bring it up with you, you seemed angry, like it was none of my business, so I dropped it.

"But the letter from the university today let me know we are in trouble. Maybe big trouble. I'm angry about my diploma, but I'm scared there are much bigger problems that you've been keeping from me. I don't want you to have to deal with all the pressure for this; it's not fair to you. This impacts both of us, and we need to deal with it as a couple. I want whatever it is to be something we tackle together."

When you take this approach you make it clear you are looking for solutions and a way to address a problem or heal a rift. It's not assigning a motive, blaming, or demanding. You are making a statement of the circumstances *as you experienced them.* Remember that we may not all have the same experiences of the very same event.

Choose your tone of voice intentionally in this step; it confirms a collaborative (or conciliatory) motive when done well. Any hint of sarcasm or blame will spoil the moment. *Sincere, open,* and *interested* are the intentions you want to convey. You are setting a tone that will guide the rest of the interaction. Once established, you are ready to *explore solutions together.*

Explore Solutions / Ask Questions

Exploring solutions is useful anytime you need to identify a decision, solution, or direction. It's not time to rehash who said what or place blame but an opportunity to discover a plan and an outcome you can both support. Remember, don't look back; you're not going that way.

Because the purpose of this step is to move forward *together*, you want to make this a dialogue—a *two-way* conversation. Monologues may work for late night comedians, but they are not effective in reaching genuine agreement you can both support.

It could be on topics of any kind:

- Deciding how you will celebrate the holiday as an extended family. Who, what, where, when?
- Discussing a family financial concern or options for a family vacation.
- Sharing concern and desire to move beyond a difficult or hurtful experience or resolution of a conflict or problem.

- Discussing sensitive subjects like sex, child-rearing, and even issues of how we live out our faith.

What does *explore solutions / ask questions* sound like? Let's continue our example.

"So how about we just put all the cards on the table, Rick, so we are both clear about what we're facing? I will work very hard not to let my emotions get ahead of me. I've made a list of all the information we need to discuss, like the outgoing expense items we have on a monthly basis—rent, utilities, cable, and so on. There are others I may not be aware of. I really want us to be open about this. I realize you've been carrying this all by yourself and I want to help. What do you think? Where do you want to start?"

As soon as you begin to solicit information from the other person, you've begun to move forward *together,* which is the goal.

One of the challenges in exploring solutions is that we most often prefer our own ideas. We have the greatest confidence in our solutions and feel most comfortable with them. It's important in this phase to remain open to the ideas, suggestions, and possible solutions that your mate offers. In fact, an important step is to solicit those ideas by *asking questions.* You may be surprised at the quality of ideas that surface, and the best solutions are often a combination—a little bit of yours, a little bit of what your spouse suggests, and voila! You've come up with something neither of you could have dreamed up all by yourself. It's not compromise; it's collaboration, a true sign of effective communication.

There are some bullets to dodge when exploring solutions and asking questions. Let's take look at a few.

You have growth opportunity if you find yourself launching into *prescribing a solution* quickly by sharing your ideas first. See if this sounds familiar: "Well, let me tell you my thoughts about this. First, I want you to know I'm pretty sure I can get a job on campus. That will help in paying my tuition, and second, we don't have to have a three-bedroom apartment, I've found a few smaller ones online for us to look at and that would reduce our monthly expense..." On and on, barely coming up for air. Have you ever participated in a conversation like that? It's a verbal marathon. You couldn't get a word in if you wanted to. For many of us, it's such a turnoff, we simply stop listening or trying to join the conversation.

Have you ever heard someone say, "Don't bring me problems, bring me solutions"? It sounds good at first, and coming with ideas to *add to the conversation* is helpful. But once you begin prescribing the fix, it monopolizes the conversation. Your spouse may feel it's a done deal and there's no point in offering ideas of his or her own.

It can be tempting at times to do all the talking, to try to push your solution through by telling your spouse what you think without taking time to hear from him or her. Telling is one-way communication: I talk, you listen. Instead, once you have explored possible solutions by sharing your thoughts and ideas, ask questions to draw the other person into the conversation and build a bridge to two-way dialogue, which is the purpose of this step. Your goal is to gather ideas and gain insight and understanding of your loved one's perspective, ideas, thoughts, and feelings. Hearing from the person you chose to spend life with honors the relationship, and it honors the Lord: "Submit to each other out of respect for Christ" (Ephesians 5:21). The best solutions await those willing to turn loose of their own preferences.

To create dialogue, invite your spouse in by asking questions.

There are two primary types of questions: closed and open. Closed questions are helpful in confirming specific information, as in "Are we still planning to go to lunch after church?" and "Is this a good time to talk about this?" from our first step of SPEAK. The response requires a simple yes or no. But to build dialogue, use open questions, which require response beyond a single word or two. When you ask an open question, it suggests, *I want to hear what you think; I'm open to your suggestions.* This can encourage others to share more fully.

Here's a quick tip guide to question starters:

Open Question Starters	Closed Question Starters
What	Is
How	Are
Where	Do, Did, Does
Who	Will
When	Can
Why	Would, Should, Could

In our Rick and Roxanne example, you will remember that it ended with two open questions: "What do you think?" and "Where do you want to start?" The questions become a natural segue to this portion of the conversation. Here's an example of this step, following their discussion: *What's the first and most important issue to deal with? Where do we begin?*

Ask a good open question or two, and then *stop talking.* When you are silent, it suggests to your spouse that it's his or her turn to speak. *Listen closely* without interruption; interruption often shuts others down. When we are interrupted, we can lose our train of thought, which creates frustration, and the message from the other person seems clear: "You can stop talking now. What I have to say is far more important." The Bible advises us: "Fools see their own way as right, but the wise *listen* to advice" (Proverbs 12:15, emphasis added).

Listening is not merely remaining silent. It requires far more. We hear with our ears and listen with our hearts. Taking notes can help you gather all the information and says to your mate, "What you're saying is important. I want to make sure I get it all." A great definition for listening is *the willingness to be changed by what you hear*. It requires you to set your own preferences aside and commit to a genuinely open mind and heart. That's not always easy, but it is possible. It's an act of your will and it will entirely change the game; great rewards await.

Some of what you hear may not be what you'd hoped for. The other person may have very different ideas or express upset or even anger. The challenge is to listen without looking for ways to overcome her objections or become defensive. How do you do that? The next step will help.

Acknowledge What You Hear

One of our most vital human needs is to be heard and understood. Listening can send the message *What you have to say is important to me. I hear you.* Being heard is one half of the equation; alone it is not sufficient. When working toward creating authentic solutions, we must also communicate *I understand what you are saying.*

Please note, we are not suggesting you must *agree* with what the other person is saying. It's an acknowledgment of what was said that communicates *I get it. I understand how you see the situation or circumstances and am aware of how you feel about it.* That's it. Simple. *I hear you. I get you.* It's called empathy, and it is a surefire way to connect in conversation.

Resist the temptation to judge how your spouse feels. It can be difficult, as we often have a near-instant gut reaction: *That's not right* or *It's not reasonable to feel that way.* Feelings aren't right or wrong. They just *are.* You may ask, "But what if he's being immature or selfish? Do I actually give him permission to feel that way?" Others don't *need* our permission to feel any certain way, and there is no value to our passing judgment by saying so. Judgment is a bridge burner. Put away the matches. Simply be clear that you understand what's been said.

Saying "I understand," however, is not an effective way to use empathy. Most often, "I understand" is met with a quick "No you don't." It's far more effective to respond in a way that *proves* we get it by identifying the *situation or circumstance* and the *impact or feelings* associated with it. So what's this nonjudgmental empathy sound like? For Rick and Roxanne:

- "You must have been under a lot of *pressure* from *carrying this all alone.*" (carrying this alone = situation / circumstance, pressure = impact / feelings.)
- "I can understand how *angry* you are about the *changes happening in your company.*" (changes in the company = situation / circumstance, angry = impact / feelings.)
- "I'm sorry you are *upset* that I wasn't *honest with you about our finances.*" (not honest about finances = situation, you are upset = impact / feelings.)

49

- "It sounds as though you are *confident* that we can *get back on track!*" (back on track = situation / circumstance, reassured = impact / feelings.)

Empathy is important anytime strong feelings or emotions are expressed, whether positive or negative. Understanding = connection. It's best to acknowledge what you hear as soon as you hear it. It validates for your mate that you are listening to his or her words and heart.

Once you've acknowledged the other person, move back to exploring solutions by asking questions: "Since we can't pay the tuition all in one payment, how do you feel about me getting a job to help speed up that process?"

The conversation continues back and forth between exploring possible options and asking questions until some real solutions begin to surface. Once you create a plan, ask one more question, and this time use a *closed question* to confirm you are both on the same page and in agreement. It will sound something like this:

"Is this something we can both commit to?"

"So can we agree and begin working on making this happen?"

"So is this workable? Can we both be happy with it and support it fully?"

You are looking for a yes or no this time. If the answer is no, go back to exploring solutions and asking questions to discuss what's missing or not acceptable. Be patient—you will get there.

It may seem unnatural or cumbersome when you first begin to use this method, but it works. And like anything new, it takes a while to get comfortable with the process. Practice makes it easier to do. So start now!

Keep Focused on the Present, Not Past History

There is one last element to SPEAK; the K, as in *keep focused on the present, not past history*. This last element is not the last step you need to take. Rather, it is a mind-set that must be present *throughout* the discussion in order for it to produce the results you desire. Think of the upstretched "arms" of the K as the beams of a bridge, supporting the entire process.

When a current situation is reminiscent of a past experience or pattern, it can be difficult to stay focused on the present and not drift back to similar conversations. This is especially true if the conversation is an attempt to address or resolve a conflict. The enemy loves to throw the past into the mix in an attempt to derail the conversation. Be vigilant. Commit to keeping your focus on this issue, rather than dredging up old hurts: "This is what you always do!" or "Well, let's not forget what happened the last time." It will get a reaction, but not one that's productive.

A critical element of forgiveness is the determined commitment to *let it go*. The Lord instructs us to forgive others in the *same way we are forgiven by Him*: fully, completely, and without bringing it up in every conversation. Aren't you grateful for that kind of forgiveness? It's to be our pattern, but it's a rough road to travel. We'll discuss this important principle in greater detail in chapter 8.

I (Deb) can recall heading into difficult conversations where resolving conflict and addressing hurt were on the agenda. I often prepared notes to help me stay on track and not allow myself to leave a positive and peaceful path. I sometimes wrote the letters LIG at the top of my notes, which stood for *Let it go*. Don't misunderstand, I was addressing the conflict or hurt, but I wasn't bringing into the conversation every one of the assorted examples from our history together in order to make my case. If there was indeed a pattern to the problem, I would mention it, but I didn't come equipped to drag out every sin and infraction committed by the other party. It's not the pattern God established for us. Deal with today, this conversation, and this opportunity.

So, there you have it. SPEAK the truth in love. Truth without love is just a set of facts and will rarely be effective in working together toward authentic agreement. There is power in agreement. In Amos 3:3, the Word is clear that without agreement it's nearly impossible to walk this life together. As marrieds, that must be the daily commitment. You are united, one, in God's eyes. Your marriage can bring glory to God through the way you do life together. The rate of divorce even in the church is high enough that your choice to live your marriage God's way will immediately make you stand out in any crowd. And when they say, "You two are so well-matched for each other and it's clear you're happy. Boy, are you lucky," you have the perfect opportunity to share with them: it's not luck, it's God.

Make It Personal

There is one more area of communication we need to cover before we wrap up this chapter: electronic. I touched on it earlier, but let's take a few minutes for a deeper dive.

I am stunned by what I see posted on Facebook and other social media sites. Couples are dealing with their issues or conflicts, which are private matters, by taking to the airwaves to make their thoughts known to the world. In most cases, my guess is they needed an immediate outlet to make their case, and their phones were handy. I've seen some really ugly stuff, with others chiming in, friends rooting for one side or the other, and the conflict widens and involves more people. How is that helpful?

I once sat next to a man in an airport waiting area who took a call on his cell phone from his wife, asking what time he'd be home. "I'm not coming home tonight" was his terse reply. "Not tonight or any night." He proceeded to tell her he had rented an apartment in the city and was filing for divorce. Over the phone. With a half-dozen strangers feeling as though we had stumbled into a very private moment.

This was a woman he had apparently loved enough at one point to believe they'd make a life together. And now he didn't have the decency or respect necessary to end it with some level of care for her feelings. There was nothing more to the conversation. After his announcement, he simply hung up. In fairness, perhaps there'd been years of conversation, counseling, and broken commitments. I have no idea whether these were people of faith. But common decency required something more, something different than a sixty-second cell phone conversation.

The same is true for conversing through e-mail or texting; although more private, it's still ineffective. Frankly, I think it's the height of cowardice to communicate over the airwaves about a conflict or anything of a sensitive nature. It allows us to hide from the difficult issue, and we may surrender good judgment about what we say and how we say it. People say things to one another electronically that they would never say to face-to-face.

Remember, please, that a text or e-mail does not have a tone of voice until the *reader assigns it one.* And if trouble is brewing, trust me, the reader will assign it the wrong one more often than not. I recently sent a note to someone who had messaged me several hours earlier that said, "Forgive me if I didn't respond as quickly as you expected." I learned later that my sincere request was read, dripping with sarcasm, as if the real message was, "Well! FOR-GIVE ME if I didn't JUMP THE MINUTE the message arrived!" Not my intention at all, but I still had to deal with the impression it left and the irritation it caused. Sending an electronic message is intentional; sometimes the poor outcome is accidental. Don't let your electronic communications replace real conversations. Make plans to have the discussion face-to-face. It will save you a world of problems.

One of the heroes in our life and marriage is author and teacher Dr. Edwin Cole. His no-nonsense take on marriage has helped us stay centered over the years. Dr. Cole taught us, "When communication ceases, abnormality sets in."

Ready to prepare your battle plan to take this communication challenge head-on? Use the resource section on the next few pages to do that. Let's put on the gloves!

Put on the Gloves! Chapter 4

If possible, we recommend both spouses complete this entire section. Respond to the questions individually, and then come together for a discussion. If you are completing this process alone, record your thoughts to the questions and use the conversation starters for a discussion with your spouse. Record what each of you shares in the "He said / She said" section.

1. How would you rate your current level of communication skill on a scale of 1 to 10 with 1 as very unskilled and 10 as highly skilled? What do you need to **start** doing? **Stop** doing? **Continue**? Think about the elements of SPEAK to guide your rating.

2. How would you rate your spouse's current level of communication skill on a scale of 1 to 10 with 1 as very unskilled and 10 as highly skilled? What would be the most helpful thing your spouse could **start** doing when communicating with you? **Stop** doing? **Continue**? Use the elements of SPEAK to guide your rating.

He Said / She Said

Use these questions to build a discussion with your spouse. Then each enter your thoughts in a "He Said / She Said" section of your journal.

- How did you rate my communication effectiveness? What things do you see that led to that rating?
- Tell me about the Start, Stop, and Continue you identified for me. Why those three?
- What steps can we take to make our faith more present in the way we deal with conflict?

God Said

Read these passages of Scripture and discuss.

"For the word of God is alive and powerful. It is sharper than the sharpest *two-edged sword*, cutting between soul and spirit, between joint and marrow. It exposes our innermost thoughts and desires" (Hebrews 4:12 NLT, emphasis added).

"I listen to their conversations and don't hear a word of truth. Is anyone sorry for doing wrong? Does anyone say, 'What a terrible thing I have done'? No! All are running down the path of sin as swiftly as a horse galloping into battle!" (Jeremiah 8:6 NLT)

"Let your conversation be gracious and attractive so that you will have the right response for everyone" (Colossians 4:6 NLT).

God hears every word we say, as well as those we think. What would he have to say about the quality of the conversation in your relationship? How well does it reflect His presence in your marriage?

New Discoveries / How Can We Use This Information?

Be specific! Write in your journal what stands out to you from this chapter.

Prayer

Lord, we acknowledge the importance of words. You spoke the worlds into existence with the words "Light, be" (Genesis 1:3, author's paraphrase). Our words, as we confess Jesus as Lord, graft us into the body of Christ. Words matter. James 3:5 reminds us that words have the power to bring life to our marriage—or destroy it. It's our desire to use words that will develop and not destroy our relationship. Holy Spirit, we ask you to guard our hearts and guide our mouths that we might bring life, not death through the words we choose. Thank You, Lord for helping us grow our skills to more productively serve you. We will take responsibility for our conversation and communication and dedicate ourselves to make our words pleasing to you and to each other.

CHAPTER 5

The Keys to Conflict Styles

"Have you told him how you feel about the situation? Does he understand how upset you are?" Sue looked up at me. Tears filled her eyes, threatening to spill over at any moment.

"No, I can't really figure out what to say. I've never been good at this stuff. I don't want to rock the boat."

"Why not?" I asked. "He's sure rocking yours. He's about to make this big decision, and he doesn't even know it's breaking your heart."

The tears breached the brim of her lids and poured freely. Silent, she nodded.

"I'm not talking about exploding, but I hope you will discuss it with him." I sensed that, although Sue agreed with me, she felt it would be wasted effort. Maybe she was right. She knew her hubby better than I did, but I pressed on.

"You are really upset. You drove off in the car, phoned me, and

DON'T GO TO BED ANGRY

asked me to meet you here for coffee. And he has *no idea* there's a problem or why you left the house. How will all of this get resolved?" I didn't have personal experience with this particular approach to marital conflict.

"We'll both be polite this evening. We will go to bed with little conversation. And in the morning, there will be an implied truce ... and we'll do it his way. It will be fine. Really. It's fine."

FINE = Feelings Inside Not Expressed. *Don't make a big deal. It'll blow over.* I couldn't disagree more, and I could never do it.

Avoidance Is Not a Path to Peace

How is it possible that the person you thought was your soul mate could be unwilling to hear your heart? For a lot of marrieds, the reason is simple: lack of practice.

After forty years of marriage, we don't struggle with this issue. We express ourselves. Sometimes loudly. We call them our *moments of intense fellowship*. We work through it and it's over. On with life.

It would be easy for me to assume my friend's husband is a control freak and that he's domineering. It's truly not the case—and that's according to his wife. She finds it so difficult, so uncomfortable to enter into any kind of discussion where disagreement or conflict is possible that she simply refuses to go there. She defers to him on decisions. She goes along to get along.

Until. Until it builds up and she passes the point of rational discussion. She doesn't trust herself to have the conversation and worries she will blow up. So she simply removes herself from the situation. Her husband is aware there's something wrong, but his previous attempts over the years to get her to open up have worn him

60

out and he no longer tries. He rides it out until the storm passes. Just as she does.

Another dear friend, Josh, had a wife who suffered in silence. She was naturally quiet, almost shy. She had come from a broken home and marital conflict terrified her. He took the lead in the relationship and rarely consulted her. So she held her tongue, kept the peace, and pressed the upset out of sight. Until the day, nearly twenty years later, she found her voice and spoke with clarity and conviction: "I don't love you anymore. I'm filing for divorce."

His pleas for counseling were ignored. She was done. Josh was devastated; his voice was barely audible as he told us the story. "She had a list of the hurts and transgressions that had occurred over the years. There was no way to undo all of it as far as she was concerned."

Their marriage posed as peaceful but lacked any true intimacy. An imitation of unity with no emotion. The needle had been on empty for a long, long time.

We Confront Because We Love

Our pastor, Alan Smith, delivered a knockout message on the true, God-given purpose for speaking up, confronting a person or an issue when needed. Our friends in the previous examples were not willing or able to take this step, but it's essential to healthy relationships.

Alan asked us to think for a moment about the conversation Jesus had with Peter following the Resurrection. It had been a tough few days for the disciple. Heartbroken and filled with shame, he had returned to his life as a fisherman. He'd taken some of the others with him.

When Jesus appeared to Peter, He had some direct, almost confrontational words with him. Let's look at John 21:15-17 together.

> When they finished eating, Jesus asked Simon Peter, "Simon son of John, do you love me more than these?"
>
> Simon replied, "Yes, Lord, you know I love you."
>
> Jesus said to him, "Feed my lambs." Jesus asked a second time, "Simon son of John, do you love me?"
>
> Simon replied, "Yes, Lord, you know I love you."
>
> Jesus said to him, "Take care of my sheep." He asked a third time, "Simon son of John, do you love me?"
>
> Peter was sad that Jesus asked him a third time, "Do you love me?" He replied, "Lord, you know everything; you know I love you."
>
> Jesus said to him, "Feed my sheep."

The New Living Translation of the Bible says Peter was "hurt," and the King James said he was "grieved." It was a painful moment for him.

So what was the point? Here are Pastor Alan's four points:

- We confront because we love.
- Connection is the goal of confrontation.
- Self-management is the way of confrontation.
- Are you "confrontable"?

Jesus confronted Peter because He loved him and the relationship was important to Him. He did it to restore the connection. He did it to restore Peter.

Speaking up is a risk. But the goal of connection is worth chasing, even when there might be moments of unpleasantness and hurt. But this connection is real. It's genuine. Marriage is worth fighting for.

When spouses retreat into silence, they no longer have enough hope or ambition to fight. An argument at least implies enough interest in the relationship to engage with each other. Silence is not *peace*—it says, "I give up."

So, if this sounds familiar, how's that *not rocking the boat* working for you?

"No one comes into marriage with perfect conflict resolution skills. You have to study your spouse and learn his / her language and conflict style. It takes time and effort, but it works. And it has taken me eleven years to learn even that much!" This survey response echoed what many acknowledged: we don't have it all together when we say, "I do," and it's important to learn each other's conflict style.

Conflict style? Yep. Experts have spent years of their careers researching this topic and sharing their findings with others. Ron and I have benefited a great deal from this work and believe it's been an important tool in our life together.

Styles: Survey Says!

Let's begin by looking at the big picture of survey results on this subject. We asked respondents to identify the conflict resolution style they and their spouses used most often.

There were four styles and descriptions from which they could choose. Here's where they landed:

Style	Style Description	Me	Spouse
Avoid	The avoider dislikes conflict and will avoid it whenever possible. The avoider will usually not mention an issue and will withdraw (physically and / or emotionally) if it comes up.	16%	30%
Accommodate	The accommodator is not comfortable with conflict. Will "go along to get along." All seems well, but it sometimes feels like it's not genuine.	31%	42%
Assertive	The assertive individual will actively seek to resolve conflict. He or she believes it's a healthy approach to reaching agreement and sustaining relationships.	61%	38%
Aggressive	The aggressive individual will use force to get what he or she wants. It includes bullying, threatening, or use of visible temper to gain the solution that is preferred.	4%	13%

So, as you can see, there are some gaps in the way we perceive ourselves and how we are seen by our mates. Not surprising. We often use different lenses to examine ourselves from those through which we view others.

Deb's Style Story

Ron and I started out with very different lenses; we aren't wired alike. Our family experiences as children were not at all similar. My parents seemed to have no real conflict; their brief moments of disagreement passed quickly and peacefully. Granted, as a child, I was not privy to every conversation they had, but the house wasn't very big. If they argued, they did it quietly. My only sibling was sixteen years my senior and left for college when I was a toddler and never returned to our home state. I didn't experience the typical "Give half to your brother" and "It's not your turn this time" moments that create friction.

That might all sound ideal. It was a pretty good life, but there are things I missed, things most adults have learned by the time they make their way to the front of the church in the fancy clothes. Like sharing. And putting others' desires above my own. And the reality that we don't live at Burger King—you can't always have it your way.

We became close as adults, my brother and I. He once offered a nickname for me—modeled after his favorite British comedy, *Rumpole of the Bailey*. Rumpole called his wife "She Who Must Be Obeyed." My brother suggested I might be known as "She Who Will Not Be Ignored." A bit of a force of nature, he observed, carrying others along on the wind of my passion. He was smiling when he said it, but I'm not certain it was meant as an endearment. Passion can feel a lot like pushiness to those caught up in the storm.

I like things the way I like them. (Oh, so do you, don't pretend to be so innocent!) But I can be rather insistent on how I think things should go—or so it has been suggested. In recent years, I've become more aware of this (as the number of pointer-outers in my life has increased), and God has joined them in bringing it to my attention.

I've had much to work through to make a space big enough in my life for Ron and his thoughts, his ideas, his opinions, and his very different experiences.

Ron's Style Story

Ron grew up in a blended family, his own father having left when Ron was about six. He was absent for over thirty years, until we located him. He was still not interested in a relationship with his son. Ron recalls as a child hearing the arguments between his parents, but he never knew the source of the volatility. After they divorced, his mother spoke little of his father, with one exception: whenever Ron became angry she'd say, "You're just like your dad."

"Looking back I realize it must have frightened her," Ron recalls. "But for me as a kid, it felt like a curse because I knew she had endured a lot at his hands. And now she was fearful I'd grow up to be just like him."

Eventually his mom remarried. There were three older step-brothers who accompanied Mel when he joined the family. The boys made life difficult—it was actually hellish at times. "They were bullies who brutalized me, boys without restraint, who introduced the world of sex, drugs, and rock and roll into our home," Ron told me. "My mom and stepdad argued often about the boys. We lived on pins and needles much of the time."

Fearful that her children would end up in real danger, Ron's mom took her children to church. She knew it was the only thing available to make a difference in their lives. And it did. All three received Christ as their Savior and began to see the potential their lives held beyond their circumstances. Life was still tense much of the time, as the alcoholism of Ron's stepdad governed how the family lived and interacted—with the exception of Sunday services and youth group to look forward to. Once Ron's mother returned to her faith, she ceased engaging in conflict with her husband.

"I think she didn't want to create any kind of barrier that would prevent him from coming to Christ," Ron speculates. "She wanted to be a good example so she simply no longer participated in arguments. She taught her kids to do the same. We worked hard to stay off Mel's radar.

"My mom had her hands full trying to keep the wheels from falling off, working to keep the family together. I love her and admire that she never gave up on Mel, praying and believing that he would someday come to Christ. He did, and they spent two really great years together before his death. The transformation was awe-inspiring."

So at seventeen when we fell in love and nineteen when we married, we were two kids, poorly prepared for so many things we'd face together, including how to resolve conflict effectively. We loved each other, we both loved Jesus, but beyond that we had no positive models to help us deal with marital conflict and no idea where or how to begin learning those lessons.

Why share our stories? Because friends over the years have assumed we were well prepared, emotionally sound, and spiritually mature the day we wed. "You were so lucky to find your soul mate!" We *are* incredibly grateful to have found each other. But prepared? Nothing could be further from the truth. We had to do as our respondent suggested: learn each other's conflict style, study God's Word, and then craft a life together through commitment and hard work that would honor our covenant and our heavenly Father. At forty years, we are very much in love and still like each other as well. It doesn't mean we live conflict-free lives. It means we have learned to use conflict more often than not as a means of discovery and avoided the damage it can bring.

Let's examine conflict styles and learn how to use this information to our benefit.

Four Conflict Styles

Numerous conflict models are designed to help us understand our wiring when it comes to resolution approaches or styles. While I (Deb) have used various models in my leadership development work in the last thirty years, the Runde-Flanagan Conflict Model stands out for us. We are confident in the supporting research and believe that it's best suited to interpersonal conflict situations, like those that occur in marriage.

When dealing with conflict, there is no one-size-fits-all method to successful resolution. But there are three critical elements that will assist you as you navigate the whitewater of conflict resolution:

> 1. Recognition of your own natural default "response to conflict"—the way you behave most often when you are under fire.
> 2. Awareness and use of conflict resolution strategies, such as communication, trust, transparency, and so on.
> 3. The willingness to invite God into the equation

to assist you in selecting the best strategy, regardless of your own internal wiring.

The work of Craig Runde and Tim Flanagan identifies four approaches to conflict resolution measured as either active or passive and constructive or destructive. The graphic below is based on their work, with some slight modifications in the descriptors.

	CONSTRUCTIVE	DESTRUCTIVE
ACTIVE	ASSERTIVE Expresses Emotions Takes in Perspectives Creates Solutions Reaches Out	AGGRESSIVE Win at All Costs Displays Anger Demeans Others Retaliates
PASSIVE	ACCOMMODATING Reflective Thinker Delays Responding Adapts	AVOIDING Yields Hides Emotions Self-Critical Withdraws

If the approach is both active and constructive, it's described as assertive. Passive and constructive action results in an accommodating approach to resolving conflict. While on the destructive side you find the polar opposites of aggressive and avoiding, depending on whether it's passive or active.

Let's define each of these styles a bit further.

AVOIDING

The avoider doesn't pursue self-concerns and does not address those of the other individual. This person does not deal with the conflict. Avoiding might take the form of diplomatically sidestepping an issue or dodging the conversation altogether. The individual may withdraw, either physically or emotionally (or both) from the situation. "I don't want to talk about it" is the avoider's anthem.

ACCOMMODATING

When accommodating, the individual ignores his or her own preferences or concerns to satisfy the other person; there is an element of self-sacrifice in this mode. Accommodating might take the form of selfless generosity or charity or following another person's lead when you would prefer not to. *Obliging, compliant,* or *long-suffering* may describe this person. "Whatever you want is okay with me" is the mantra for the accommodator.

AGGRESSIVE

The aggressor pursues self-concerns or self-interest at the other person's expense. This is a power-oriented mode in which the aggressor uses whatever power seems appropriate to win a position: the ability to argue, his or her position or rank, or withholding resources ranging from affection to finances. Competing includes behavior described as *forceful, insistent,* or *hard-hitting.* "I will win no matter the cost!" is the aggressor's battle cry.

ASSERTIVE

An assertive approach involves an attempt to work with another to find some solution that *fully satisfies* both their concerns. It means digging into an issue to pinpoint the underlying needs and wants of the two individuals. When using an assertive approach, two people might explore a difference or disagreement to learn from each other's perspectives in order to discover a creative solution to an interpersonal problem. "Look what we can do when we work together!" is the theme song for the assertive individual.

As you read through the four styles you can probably identify the behaviors that you demonstrate most often at times of conflict. And if you can't, I'll bet your spouse can!

Which is the best approach? Whether passive or active, the positive (left) half of the graphic should be considered the sunny side of the street. An assertive approach requires the willingness to share your emotions and listen to the perspective of others, which may not be easy. But when coupled with reaching out to others to create solutions, it's easy to understand why it may be the most powerful approach of all.

Is it ever wise to delay responding? If the level of emotion is so high that escalation of the conflict is a certainty, taking a brief time-out to cool down could be the only way to peacefully achieve agreement. The Bible seems to agree: "Hotheads stir up conflict, but patient people calm down strife" (Proverbs 15:18). Take a quick break to allow tempers to calm a bit, but we suggest setting a time frame both will return to the conversation. That ensures the issue will be resolved, not just swept aside to erupt again another day.

Little hope can be assigned to the approaches found on the destructive side, whether active or passive. The aggressive approach of "win at all costs" is not better or worse than the passive preference to withdraw and hide emotions. One's louder than the other, but both create hurt, resentment, and anger (even if never expressed) over time. And both have potential to damage the relationship.

Recognizing the pattern of your conflict response and that of your mate is an important first step in proactively and productively managing it, first individually and then as a couple.

Can Two Styles Make One Strong Marriage?

Where do these default styles come from? Some may be the result of the models and life experiences we've had with conflict. Think back to our stories. I (Deb) experienced little conflict growing up, which left me unprepared to deal with it effectively. Ron experienced a great deal of conflict but was required to keep it under wraps in order to stay off the radar. He, too, had little practice and was unprepared to resolve it when it occurred. But it did occur.

Where do we land on the style sorter? Neither of us could ever be described as passive. After years of being silenced, Ron found his voice. I never lacked one. We are both strongly opinionated, comfortable expressing our thoughts and feelings. We can be passionate about what we believe. That leaves us only two options: assertive or aggressive.

Our primary style is assertive. We are able to discuss our differences and disagree agreeably the vast majority of the time. The discovery of a new approach to a situation or a solution that comes from our combined dialogue is most often the happy result. We rarely have conflict over anything important; those issues came into alignment a long time ago. But there are times we find ourselves thinking, *I can't believe he doesn't see this!* or *I just don't think she understands what I'm saying!* Those are the occasions that *passion* can cross the line to *push* and we find ourselves fighting each other in the ring. Forty years and we still fall prey to the enemy at times.

Some of it may be our internal wiring, the way our brains work. The keys to our default conflict style may live deep somewhere in the brain. But regardless of where our styles originate, there is good news. God has known us since before we were in our mothers' wombs. He made us. And when we became grafted into His family through Christ Jesus, His Word says we were made *new*. "This means that anyone who belongs to Christ has become a new person. The old life is gone; a new life has begun!" (2 Corinthians 5:17 NLT). He didn't just clean us up. He made us *new*.

But it's a choice—one we must make daily—to walk in the new life we received when we gave our lives to Christ. God gave the Holy Spirit to remind us of all the things that Jesus taught, to remind us of His instruction. And God's Spirit empowers us to resist the temptation to indulge in anger or withdrawal, but to actively and constructively resolve the conflict.

One of the survey statistics we mentioned in chapter 2 was the answer to this question: "If you identified yourself as a Christian, what role does your faith play in the way you and your spouse manage conflict in your marriage?" Some 58 percent responded that they incorporated their beliefs into their conflict resolution process. What are the remaining 42 percent doing? Going it alone? Making it up as they go along? Consulting Oprah and Dr. Phil?

A verse Ron and I have taken to heart is 1 Corinthians 10:13. Although it is familiar, we were married for many years before we fully understood this Scripture and the promise it provides: "No temptation has overtaken you except what is common to humanity. God is faithful, and He will not allow you to be tempted beyond what you are able, but with the temptation He will also provide a way of escape so that you are able to bear it" (HCSB).

Look carefully at the words, "but with the temptation." At the *very moment* we are tempted to step outside of godly behavior during conflict, the Lord provides us a way of escape! Picture yourself trapped in a burning building. At the exact moment it seems you will have to jump from the fortieth-floor window, a firefighter appears with a respirator and the lifeline to safety. All you have to do is follow him out of the path of certain destruction.

That's what the Lord does for us.

When you find yourself in the throes of conflict that seeks to suck the life out of your relationship with each other and the Lord, stop. Stop long enough to ask, *How does God see me in this moment? What does He think of my behavior?* At our house, asking those questions has often been enough to cut the crazy short. The wake-up call that occurs in that moment has often taken the wind right out of our indignant sails. Jesus suffered and died to secure our lives. *How could we treat each other so carelessly?*

We are not stuck with our combined experiences to define our life as a couple; God has transformed our individual lives into one flesh. He has already created something unique in the process that never existed before. But He goes well beyond that as He guides and directs us through His Word and cheers us on when we get it right. He corrects us and instructs us when we get it wrong. We are not on our own. *He is a good, good Father.*

Let's put on the gloves and step into the ring. We've got work to do.

PUT ON THE GLOVES! CHAPTER 5

If possible, we recommend both spouses complete this entire section. Respond to the questions individually, and then come together for a discussion. If you are completing this process alone, record your thoughts to the questions and use the conversation starters for a discussion with your spouse. Record what each of you shares in the "He said / She said" section.

1. What is your conflict style as described in this chapter? What factors do you believe created the approach you use most often?

2. How does your belief in Christ appear in the moments of conflict you and your spouse experience? Are you living as a new creation? What steps can you take to make that a reality?

HE SAID / SHE SAID

Use these questions to build a discussion with your spouse. Then each enter your thoughts in a "He Said / She Said" section of your journal.

- How do our styles help or hinder us?
- How can we become more aware of them when the conversation is starting to go south on us?
- What steps can we take to walk fully in the reality of the "way of escape" God provides?

GOD SAID

"No temptation has overtaken you except what is common to humanity. God is faithful, and He will not allow you to be tempted beyond what you are able, but with the temptation He will also provide a way of escape so that you are able to bear it" (1 Corinthians 10:13 HCSB).

What does this Scripture mean in the moment you are tempted? What steps will you need to take to avoid the temptation for anger or withdrawal, or even going along to get it over with?

READ THIS SCRIPTURE TOGETHER AND DISCUSS

"The weapons we fight with are not the weapons of the world. On the contrary, they have divine power to demolish strongholds" (2 Corinthians 10:4 NIV).

- What strongholds do you need to fight in your marriage?
- What issues resurface again and again that need to be demolished once and for all?

NEW DISCOVERIES / HOW CAN WE USE THIS INFORMATION?

Be specific! Write in your journal what stands out to you from this chapter.

PRAYER

Thank you, Lord, for being such a good, good Father. You cheer us on and we know you are for us. We submit the experiences of our lives, both before we married and as husband and wife, and ask that you show us how to walk in peace with each other, regardless of our past experience. Please bring us greater awareness of who we are in you: new, not remodeled, made to bring you honor and glory in our lives. Help us to yield our hearts and our conversation to the nudge of the Holy Spirit, so your light may be visible through our marriage to a lost and hungry world.

CHAPTER 6
COMMUNICATION TRAPS

In previous chapters we explored the importance of developing and using effective communication skills. When we have the right tools we can move forward to tackle our differences. And when we work together, we get the job done with outcomes we can both support. Without them, we're caught in an unproductive and negative cycle. The lack of communication skills doesn't keep us from talking, but we spin with frustration and anger, so we're no closer to a solution than we were before the discussion began. In the process, we've done some damage to each other. Good skills are vital.

Just as important as building good skills is the need to identify the communication traps that trip us up—especially when we are caught up in conflict. These traps become barriers that prevent us from using conflict constructively. They are also roadblocks to intimacy and closeness.

We will explore four barriers that antagonize, paralyze, and minimize the potential to reach a positive solution in a positive way. The communication traps we will cover are:

1. Silence
2. Sulking
3. Sarcasm
4. Sound

Each of these behaviors is a form of punishment applied in order to get what we want. "If you won't do what I want you to do, then I will (fill in the behavior here)." That's called *manipulation*. Every trap on our list is a form of manipulation. Manipulation can be defined as controlling or playing upon someone by artful, unfair, or insidious means, especially to one's own advantage.

Manipulation is about getting what you want at the expense of another. What does the Bible say about it? It's a long list, but let's hit a couple of the highlights:

- "Don't do anything for selfish purposes, but with humility think of others as better than yourselves. Instead of each person watching out for their own good, watch out for what is better for others" (Philippians 2:3-4).
- "No one should look out for their own advantage, but they should look out for each other" (1 Corinthians 10:24).

These aren't optional suggestions; the scriptures are strongly worded: "Don't do" and "No one should." It's clear that manipulation does not reflect our new birth in Christ and is unacceptable for us as believers—*and as husband and wife*. We'll continue to discuss this topic as we move through the chapter.

Perhaps you are the one who must deal with your spouse's use of one or more of these approaches. Or maybe you are the mate who doles it out. We'll begin by reviewing the strategies to help move both of you to a healthier place. This will allow us to look through the lens of solution as we learn about each trap.

If your spouse engages in any (or many) of these communication traps, you are left to deal with the behavior and the potential damage to the relationship it brings. Let's talk about how to handle the traps effectively.

DEALing with the Traps

We will use the four letters of DEAL as a way to remember a proactive approach as you work to free yourself (and your loved one) from one of these traps.

> **D**—**Don't** take the bait.
> **E**—**Explain** the impact of the behav-
> ior and **express** your expectations.
> **A**—**Ask** questions to draw your
> spouse into dialogue.
> **L**—**Let go** of the need to manage
> your mate's behavior. Manage
> your own.

We'll review each element in detail for those who must deal with their loved one's use of the communication traps. Let's start at the top of the list.

DON'T TAKE THE BAIT

The goal of manipulation is to hook the other party into doing something that serves one's own purpose, regardless of the impact on the other person. When the bait is dangled on that hook, the goal is to get you to bite, to react in the moment. So whether your mate doles out silence or volume, sarcasm or vindictiveness, your objective is to *respond, not react*. What's the difference? A *response* is a thoughtful, purposeful reply, considered and chosen according to your faith and your relationship with your spouse and God. A *reaction* is an in-the-moment reply based more on emotions such as anger, hurt, or pride. Think of it as the quick-draw retort that you (and the Lord) will regret the moment it leaves your lips.

A reaction is similar to running downhill. You start quickly, pick up momentum, and soon you're unable to manage the speed of the descent. You lose control and are subject to finish the journey however gravity defines. And you may land in a heap with some scrapes and bruising as your reward. A response requires more effort; it's the hike up the hill. It's slow, measured, and provides the opportunity to maintain your balance while continuing the progress to the top. From that vantage point, the big picture is in full view.

Considering how you choose to reply is useful because it may reveal ways you give your partner attention when he or she indulges in one of the communication traps. A reaction is one step closer to taking the bait, which you want to avoid. Instead, respond. Let's look at an example to help clarify the difference between responding and reacting.

Let's say that your spouse has made a purchase beyond the amount that either of you can make without checking with each other. It's something you have agreed upon as a couple, but your spouse has disregarded the commitment and exceeded that limit several times recently. Here's an example of the difference between a reaction and a response:

Reaction: "I can't believe you just continue to ignore the spending limit! You go ahead and do whatever you want and always think *I'm* making a big deal when you do it. It's childish. You obviously think the rules apply only to me."

Response: "I want to talk with you about the new flat screen TV you bought today. It's over the limit we agreed on and required a discussion before moving ahead. I'd like to discuss it. Would now be a good time for that conversation?"

It's clear that the first reply, the *reaction*, will often sound like an attack to the offending party. When we feel attacked, it's natural to respond with one of two approaches: return the favor and launch a counterattack or get defensive. Both responses are human; neither choice breeds the potential for a peaceful discussion that yields a positive outcome.

The *response* is the approach that avoids the quick one-two punch of blame and accusation. It includes a clear statement of both the issue as well as the desire to discuss the situation and seeks permission to have that conversation. The possibility to achieve a solution and avoid damage to the relationship is preserved.

Explain the Impact of the Behavior and Express Your Expectations

The next step is to help your spouse recognize and understand the impact on you as a result of the communication trap. Part of that process is to express your expectations as the conversation continues. For example, if your spouse uses excess volume to make the point in an attempt to overpower you and push your concern aside, it's important to respond appropriately. Here is how that response might sound: "Making the purchase outside of our commitment not only disregards the agreement we made, but *I* feel disregarded too. It's a trust issue. It sends the message that my thoughts and feelings are not important to you, which I resent a great deal. We need to talk about this, but I will expect you to discuss it respectfully without yelling at me, which is unacceptable."

Once the impact is explained, and expectations for continuing the conversation are established, you are ready to move ahead. To do that, you will engage your spouse in the discussion.

Ask Questions to Draw Your Spouse into Dialogue

Open-ended questions require more than a shrug, nod, or simple one-word answer. Recalling the conversation starters in chapter 2 will help get you started. The purpose of this part of the discussion is to draw your spouse into solution-building, with the goal of a joint decision. Continuing our example, it may sound like this:

- "If the positions were reversed, how would you feel? What message would you take from it had I been the spender today?"
- "Help me understand why you decided it was acceptable to step beyond our spending limit without having a conversation with me first?"
- "How do we keep this from continuing? What steps can we take to insure there are no more surprises?"

You may discover information you were unaware of, changing the way you view the issue. Or not. Either way, you are beginning the work of building a solution together. Eventually, steps will surface and you can begin to create a plan. The final question may sound like this:

"Are you committed to the steps we've identified?"

Please note the final question is a closed-ended one: "Are you committed to the steps...?" Once you've worked through the discussion, this is appropriate. You have arrived at a decision point and it's time to come to agreement. If the answer is yes, you can decide on specific methods to support follow-through the next time. If the answer is no, go back and ask additional questions to help move you and your mate closer to an acceptable outcome you can both live with. This may be a back-and-forth conversation rather than a one-and-done kind of deal. Be patient and remember, you manage you, let your spouse do the same. Which brings us to the final element of DEALing with the trap.

LET GO OF THE NEED TO CONTROL YOUR MATE'S BEHAVIOR. MANAGE YOUR OWN

This conversation is not about me controlling you. I'm here to control me. Even if you never verbalize this, don't ever forget it. We have our hands full trying to manage our own behavior. You can recalibrate the tone and direction of the conversation if you remember this simple principle.

When your mate hits below the belt by using one of the communication traps, there may be a tendency to try to manage or control his or her behavior. It's important to remember your first priority is to give your spouse insight into how that behavior impacts you. It's best done with an attitude that says, *I'm here to give you helpful information about me and how this affected me. And I'm certain if you knew how this makes me feel, you'd never want me to experience that.* This approach gives the spouse the benefit of the doubt, which helps minimize the potential offense and moves the couple forward.

So now that we have a plan in place to DEAL with the traps, let's begin by exploring the first on the list: Silence.

The Traps: Approaches That Tear Us Apart

TRAP NO. 1: SILENCE

"Silence is golden" may be a nice sentiment, and sometimes remaining quiet is helpful. For example, if one or both of you are too upset to address the issue without letting your emotions direct the traffic, take a brief time-out until cooler heads prevail. It will save you time and emotion in the long run.

In the midst of conflict, prolonged silence is a dangerous communication tool. The silent treatment—withdrawing and refusing to engage in any conversation at all—is destructive.

"It's the most common pattern of conflict in marriage or any committed, established romantic relationship," says Paul Schrodt, PhD, professor and graduate director of communication studies at Texas Christian University. "And it does tremendous damage."

Schrodt led a meta-analysis of seventy-four studies, including more than fourteen thousand participants. A meta-analysis combines and contrasts results from different studies on the same topic to identify patterns on a broader spectrum. According to Schrodt, the demand / withdraw pattern occurs when one spouse makes what seems like a demand (which is often no more than a request or suggestion) and the other spouse withdraws or retreats into silence. Frustration grows as the refusal to communicate continues over time.

Schrodt's research shows couples who use this approach routinely report low satisfaction with their relationships, less intimacy, and poorer communication than those who do not select this response. The damage can be emotional and physical: emotional effects are such things as anxiety and aggression; physical damage shows up as symptoms of anxiety, such as headache and digestive problems.

The demand / withdraw pattern is also a very hard pattern to break. We've known couples who could go three or four days without speaking to each other. As a couple, we don't have that kind of self-discipline. Sooner or later, we'd find it necessary to remind each other about taking out the trash or making the bank deposit. It's just not a helpful approach and requires an incredible level of self-discipline to maintain. If you have that much self-control, we'd suggest you have the ability to manage your conversation in a productive manner from the beginning.

Why do some choose to suffer in silence instead of getting to a solution? Shutting a partner out is a powerful way to convey dissatisfaction or displeasure: *Let me be clear: I'm not happy and I'm particularly unhappy with you.* It's even more powerful if the silent one is lavishing conversation and positive attention on others while giving you the cold shoulder.

The silent treatment is a passive-aggressive action. Remaining "silent" is never actually a silent act since it "speaks" in other ways. It achieves a very important objective: it provides the spouse the assurance he or she is hurting or punishing the other person. There may also be a feeling of power from creating uncertainty over how long the "silence" will last. This is one more form of manipulation.

The silent treatment may have been learned from childhood— part of the baggage someone drags along. But if the mate engages in this behavior regularly as a grown-up, it is a *deliberate choice.* This is important to remember if you are prone to try and "fix" issues in the relationship or if you feel you have done something to cause the other to withdraw.

Fixers may go into action to remedy the situation when their partners freeze them out. They often try to:

- jolly their spouses out of it.
- provide extra positive attention.
- offer sympathy.
- spoil them (for example, by cooking their favorite meals or suggesting a movie they want to see).
- grab their attention and shock them into response by being abusive or aggressive.
- request others to intervene on their behalf (including friends or children).
- wait until the thaw, and then freeze *them* out with the silent treatment as retaliation.

If your spouse is the strong, silent type, what happens upon coming out of the deep-freeze phase? Do you discuss it and if so, how? Are you left feeling blamed, or does your spouse take responsibility and ask forgiveness? Is the silence discussed, or do you simply resume life because you're glad to have your partner back? These are important questions to consider and address.

Once the thaw has occurred and you are able to discuss and decide on a solution, help your mate understand your expectation for the future. That is, the next time you are frozen out you will acknowledge the upset but will leave him or her alone until conversation resumes. No begging or pleading, and no going on as though nothing is wrong. This is not a form of punishment; it's a statement of the consequence of your partner's behavior you are no longer willing to reward. It's our nature to gravitate to the reward; when it's absent, we often move away from the behavior. That's the goal: to help your mate recognize the silent treatment will not be effective going forward. You are breaking the cycle of the past and pointing the way toward better conversations for both of you.

In some cases, talking it through is enough to help a partner understand the upsetting impact of his or her actions. For others, it may take a few instances of standing your ground for your spouse to realize silence is not going to achieve his or her desired results any longer. This puts the ball in your partner's court and he or she must make a choice: continue with an unsuccessful approach, or take a more productive path.

In theory, dealing with this kind of behavior is simple. In practice it can be very difficult, as it will take time for you to unlearn your usual reactions, just as it will take time for your partner to stop the silent treatment as a means of communication and control. In fact you may face resistance to your efforts to break the pattern and your partner may leave the discussion, retreating into silence once more. Follow through on your stated expectation; allow some space. Use the time to pray for your mate and for the relationship. Be cordial and open to any indication of the thaw. Allow your spouse to make the first move and greet it warmly.

In his study, Dr. Schrodt's observation of which spouse retreats more often is interesting. "One of the most important things we found is that even though wife-demand / husband-withdraw occurs more frequently, it's not more or less damaging," he says. No matter what role each partner plays, it's the pattern itself that's the problem. "It's a real, serious sign of distress in the relationship."

It's perhaps the toughest trap on the list, but we can't remain silent on the silent treatment. Let's move on to the second communication trap.

TRAP NO. 2: SULKING

We often associate sulkiness with kids who don't get their way. Some adults are just taller two year olds; it's still their go-to behavior when differences surface. How does sulkiness present? Here are a few descriptors: glum, mopey, pouty, or sullen; grumbling with a half-suppressed or muttered complaint. Often it's under the breath, just loud enough so the person to whom it's directed can *almost* make it out.

Dealing with a mopey or pouty partner is a chore. We often feel as though we need to cheer the person up, and pull him or her over to the sunny side of the street. But again, remember, when a mate is sulky, it's a chosen behavior. Use the four elements of DEAL to address the behavior. For our purposes, we are going to focus on one specific aspect of sulking: that muttered complaint, also known as murmuring. God is not a big fan of murmuring.

Murmuring and grumbling kept the Israelite children from crossing into the Promised Land. After all they had seen the Lord do—delivering them from slavery in Egypt, performing miracles on their behalf again and again—they continued to grumble and complain on a daily basis. Finally, the Lord had enough.

You can read the account in Numbers 14 ending with God's declaration: "You will not enter and occupy the land I swore to give you. The only exceptions will be Caleb son of Jephunneh and Joshua son of Nun" (Numbers 14:30 NLT). It was a big price to pay for what some might today characterize as just expressing their opinions.

The specific charge made against the Israelites was that the murmuring focused on God's plan and the men tasked with carrying it out. When grumbling and murmuring against a spouse, we "separate what God joined together." Sound familiar? Our wedding covenant as husband and wife is God's plan. We are made one flesh, joined together in the Lord. Murmuring about one's spouse dances dangerously close to lodging a complaint against God's plan.

We're not suggesting that agreement and alignment are automatic when we marry or that God won't tolerate us discussing differences with our mates. But murmuring is that sulky, covert, almost undercover complaint that comes at the other person from the side and can take us down without warning.

The New Testament continues to warn the believer of the dangerous effect of murmuring.

"Do all things without murmurings and disputings: That ye may be blameless and harmless, the sons of God, without rebuke, in the midst of a crooked and perverse nation, among whom ye shine as lights in the world; holding forth the word of life" (Philippians 2:14-16 KJV). In other words, when we fall prey to the trap of murmuring, we are *not blameless* and we *fail to shine* as lights in a dark and dying world.

While it destroys our ability to stand as a testament to God, murmuring will also do damage to the intimacy of a marriage. Covert communication like murmuring hides behind the lowered voice. "I didn't catch that. What did you say?" is met with "Oh, it was nothing." Oh there was something—just not something said with the goal of transparent discussion. If you are married to one who murmurs, it keeps you in the dark, with the uneasy feeling that *something's not right here.*

Why is murmuring an approach some select?

- Perhaps they grew up in homes where expressing their opinions was punished.
- Some may dislike confrontation but feel the need to express dissatisfaction at some level, perhaps hoping they will then be solicited for more information.
- Maybe they've experienced dismissal, judgment, or rejection for sharing their thoughts.

Whateverthe reason may be, if you constantly encounter that behavior, it can wear you out. In some cases, the nonmurmuring spouse simply gives up and ignores it, which often brings great dissatisfaction for the mate. The murmuring was, after all, a message, even if indirect.

How do you deal with it? Address it! Follow the four steps to DEAL with it and put you and your partner on a collaborative and open path. It might sound like this: "Babe, I know there's something on your mind, something that's bothering you. You've been sulking—grumbling and quietly complaining—but you're not addressing the issues directly. It bothers me; it makes me feel as though you don't trust me or have enough confidence in our relationship to bring it up for discussion. I think it's important for us to be open with each other, not dropping hints or making little remarks just out of earshot. I love and care about you. If it's bothering you, it's important to me. I'd like us to talk about whatever it is that's upsetting you. What's going on?"

This approach is not guaranteed to immediately loosen the lips, but it communicates everything the complainer / murmurer needs to be reassured of: *I love you,* and *If it's important to you, it's important to me.*

As the discussion continues, focus on managing your own behavior with a goal of response, not reaction.

If you're the one who sulks, look at it from your spouse's perspective. If you adopt the role of the child, what role does it leave for your mate? *Parent.* Oh, ick. It's certainly not the picture of two godly adults, who are able to "shine as lights in the world, holding forth the word of life."

When you are unhappy and tempted to sulk and get pouty, remember that God's presence and power are able to help us cope with any issue, problem, or difficulty without the need to murmur. The Holy Spirit was given to guide us into all truth and can certainly empower us to raise discussion with our spouses as adults, not children. Murmuring is always an approach God will reject. As Paul wrote in 1 Corinthians 10:5-10, murmuring was one of the five sins that kept an entire generation of the Israelites from achieving their maximum potential in the Lord. Is your marriage achieving its maximum potential?

Expressing discontent is not only acceptable, it is *required* in marriage to keep the lines of communication open. As long as we keep our attitudes and conversation constructive and aligned with God's Word, there is opportunity for a positive outcome.

Tips to keeping your conversation constructive:

- **Pray.** It is possible to complain to God without losing sight of His sovereignty, acknowledging that He may choose a different reality for us than we had hoped for. Murmuring may not be about your spouse, but a situation or circumstance. If your job is draining you, complaining about it constantly, pouting, and grumbling will take a toll on the atmosphere in your relationship. Don't require your spouse to fix what perhaps God is better equipped to do.

- **Speak up!** If your mate's new job opportunity would require a move to another state, which is not your preference, discuss it openly with him or her. Don't drop pouty hints or sulk. Share your concerns and feelings about the situation in an adult manner. Pray about the decision together, asking God to make the right choice clear to both of you. And if it doesn't go your way, don't sulk! Ask God to change your heart and help you move forward as a couple.

You can do this! Don't be locked out of your "Promised Land" because you are unable to step up and leave sulking behind. It's time to grow up. "When I was a child, I used to speak like a child, reason like a child, think like a child. But now that I have become a man, I've put an end to childish things" (1 Corinthians 13:11).

TRAP NO. 3 SARCASM

I once saw a sign in a store that said, "Sarcasm is what keeps me from telling you how I really feel." So, "Wow, *great outfit*," as your wife meets you at work for lunch in jeans and flip-flops translates as *You're an embarrassing mess.*

The real message comes across loud and clear, even if it takes a moment to be deciphered. For a moment, you bask in the glow of what sounds like a nice comment, only to discover the not-so-hidden message. Being caught off-guard magnifies the insult and doubles the damage.

Though it's often camouflaged as humor, sarcasm is merely a cowardly and comfortable way for people to express emotions without actually coming out and saying what's on their minds. Some examples are:

- hurt feelings ("Gee, wasn't *that* thoughtful!")
- criticism ("The bed's not going to make itself, you know.")
- disapproval of some action ("Just what we needed, another pet in the house.")

"Just kidding" is often the defense when you call them on their use of sarcasm. Baloney. They weren't kidding and both parties know it. The smarmy, thick tone of voice announces its presence. It's intentional and it leaves a mark.

The purpose of sarcasm is to belittle one person and elevate the other. Jesus warned against such communication in Matthew 5:22: "But I say to you that everyone who is angry with their brother or sister will be in danger of judgment. If they say to their brother or sister, 'You idiot,' they will be in danger of being condemned by the governing council. And if they say, 'You fool,' they will be in danger of fiery hell." And *you idiot* is often the thinly veiled message of sarcasm.

Scripture directs us to speak the truth in love, to engage in genuine expression of our thoughts and feelings and how to do this in alignment with God's Word and character:

> Then we will no longer be immature like children. We won't be tossed and blown about by every wind of new teaching. We will not be influenced when people try to trick us with lies so clever they sound like the truth. Instead, we will speak the truth in love, growing in every way more and more like Christ, who is the head of his body, the church. (Ephesians 4:14-15 NLT)

Lies that sound like the truth: that's a great definition of sarcasm. Sarcasm is the roundhouse punch to the gut. And if exposed often enough to this pain, we may apply a thick protective shell to prevent the damage. Conversations become guarded and intimacy suffers.

When we speak something other than the truth, we fail to demonstrate the character of Christ. We represent the behavior of another—the father of lies. "When he lies, it is consistent with his character; for he is a liar and the father of lies" (John 8:44 NLT). The source of truth is light while sarcasm is rooted in darkness. Where do you want to live?

The way to avoid sarcasm is simple: speak the truth in love. Speaking the truth *requires* love; love gives truth its voice. The mature Christ follower puts away a cheap imitation of truth. It's possible to deliver a difficult message in a loving way, even if you and / or the hearer might be uncomfortable.

Putting sarcasm to rest may not be easy and it won't happen overnight; it's a habit, an autoreply, which can be hard to break. But it's worth the effort. Here are four reasons to set sarcasm aside:

- **Sarcasm is unkind.** Sarcastic people use humor, hoping it takes a bit of the edge off, but it doesn't usually blunt the blow. It's a bully tactic and wounds others.
- **Sarcasm is a form of cowardice.** Rather than expressing real feelings, sarcasm slithers in and communicates with slightly less aggression than what the person would *really* like to say, making it more acceptable in the mind of the sarcastic partner. It's not acceptable; it's a passive-aggressive punch.
- **Sarcasm is a "safe" way to pronounce judgment.** Judging others is not an assignment for the Christ-follower. Belittling your mate with the goal of making yourself look superior

is a loser tactic—and it's visible to others. Your spouse is wounded and you come off looking needy and insecure.

- **Sarcasm uses words to tear down.** Insult, put-down, slap, and slur: all are descriptive of sarcasm. There is no high purpose in sarcasm. God is clear that our words should build up, not tear down. "So let's strive for the things that bring peace and the things that build each other up" (Romans 14:19).

So if you are married to Sarcastic Sam or Suzanne, you will need to DEAL with it. Here's an example of how it might sound, using the four elements: "Sam, your sarcasm isn't funny and it really hurts. It's clear you use it try to send a message, but I can't hear it. I feel bullied and can't get past the pain. I'm willing to talk, but not unless you are willing to speak openly, without the sarcasm. What's bothering you that I need to understand? What are you trying to say?"

Remember you cannot control your spouse's behavior in this discussion. Focus on managing your own. Be mindful of who you are: "All of you are children of light and children of the day. We don't belong to night or darkness" (1 Thessalonians 5:5).

Listen for cues that the conversation is steered toward authentic communication and move forward as it does. If the sarcasm continues, you will need to withdraw from the interaction. "Sam, as I said earlier, I'm not willing to continue the discussion with sarcasm in the mix. I'm eager to work this out. Please let me know when you are ready and able to discuss it respectfully."

Remember, withdrawal is not a punishment; it's a consequence of Sam's choice to continue the destructive behavior. Do your part; be ready to return to the conversation when there is a commitment to talk without being sarcastic.

So if your honey comes home with a T-shirt that reads, "Sarcasm. Just one of the many services I offer," put it in the ragbag quickly!

Trap No. 4: Sound

I (Deb) once traveled to Mexico with Robin, a high school buddy, and her family for a weeklong vacation. After a very long drive, an hour from our destination, the car sputtered to a stop. Fortunately we were near a gas station and pushed it into the lot. I watched as Robin's dad peered beneath the hood and determined the problem. He looked triumphant. "It's just a belt. Easy fix. We'll replace it and be on our way in no time."

The jubilation was short-lived.

No one in the station spoke English. No one in our car spoke Spanish. No problem? Big problem.

Robin's dad tried desperately to make himself understood. He pointed to the area in need of the belt, but it was dark and hard to see. From the Toyota's backseat, the scene looked like a bad game of charades. He gestured with his hands, pointing to the belt around his waist. No success. Eventually, he began to amp up the volume. Louder, perhaps, would make the point and explain our need more clearly. He wore himself (and our new gas station friend) out by shouting again, and again, "Timing belt! TIMING BELT!" His anger grew as the frustration continued. Eventually, he looked a little scary.

We slept in the car that night. And I learned several important lessons:

- Volume does not improve understanding.
- Volume makes others yell back.
- Volume eventually shuts people down. They stop listening

and walk away from you and lock up their shop and go home
and leave you stranded.

- Volume may lead to sleeping in the car for the night.

The story is funny now, but at the time, not so much. Volume
created an entirely new set of issues for a group of Americans in a
Japanese car at midnight in Mexico.

When we consider sound as a communication trap, we often
think of two areas: volume and tone of voice. We discussed tone of
voice in the sarcasm section. It's not so much *what* is said but *how* it
is said. That may be familiar to most every married man and woman.
I call it *snarkasm*. It's the snarky, sometimes acidic tone of voice that
makes sarcasm so pungent.

So in this section, we'll focus on volume—delivered in a pleth-
ora of packages including yelling, hollering, and screaming. What's
the difference between them? Beats me, but they all trap us and trip
us up at just about the same rate.

Our friend Pat talked with us about the volume issues that
ended his marriage. "There was no ability to discuss a difference
of opinion that didn't begin and end with Anita yelling at me. Big
things, small things, it didn't matter. I tried all the techniques. I lowered my voice. I asked her to lower hers. I withdrew, but she simply
followed me around the house hollering the entire time. I begged, I
pleaded, and I prayed.

"I felt responsible at times and ashamed, too, that as the man of
the house I couldn't seem to keep this from happening. It's not the
kind of thing I wanted to discuss with my pastor."

He looked away briefly. "I saw the signs before we got married,
but I ignored it. Anita's mom was a yeller, too, and after a few years I

could see myself in her dad's expression when they had a big blow up. It happened once at Christmas dinner. It was awful. I used to rationalize that at least Anita never did it in front of anyone else but the kids."

It's not the life Pat expected. The couple had met in church. Both were active in small group study and outreach ministry and continued to take leadership roles in their church after they wed. "I felt like a fraud. Half the time the drive either to or from church was an outburst, yelling all the way there or home. But we could put on the church face when we needed to."

Still, Pat hung in there. "I thought love could carry us through. I was wrong."

Pat finally asked his wife to go to counseling with him. Her response was not surprising to him. "For crying out loud! I'm on the women's ministry board, Pat. There's nothing wrong with me. Our marriage is fine. It's nothing to get worked up about." It was the first time Pat felt hopeless. "I was angry too. It was impacting the kids. They walked around on pins and needles, warning me when I arrived home, 'Mom's in a bad mood.' I became resentful."

Why do some fall into the trap of volume as a communication strategy? Again, expressing anger with volume can be among the baggage we drag through life. Pat's wife learned what she had lived and brought it to the marriage where it became a barrier in the development of their relationship. To her, it was normal. For others, yelling may be triggered by a myriad of stimulators:

- Unmet expectations, whether of self or others
- Insecurity about one's ability, position, or knowledge
- Low level of self-esteem, which prods one to clamor for position or acknowledgment
- The need for control over people and situations

- Disappointment
- Threat or perceived danger
- Frustration, fatigue, or fear

Regardless of which trigger throws the switch, yelling, screaming, or shouting is a choice. It's one that Pat's wife continued to make despite the damage it caused.

After more than ten years Pat threw in the towel. "I was raised to believe you married once, forever, end of story. I felt like such a failure and my parents were so disappointed in me. In me! If it weren't so tragic, I'd laugh. It's been tough on all of us, including my ex. She's not a terrible person. She just can't control herself; it's how she was brought up. I got to the point I couldn't continue to try to do it for her. It was never successful anyway."

Human love alone is almost never enough to carry us through; maintaining a relationship with Jesus and allowing *His Spirit* to direct us is essential to living life in the image of Christ.

Self-control is the heart of the issue here and the antidote to the trap of volume. "I just can't seem to help myself" is both a potential cop-out and a true statement. When we rely on our human ability to walk in the character of Christ, we will fail every single time. "Since you have heard about Jesus and have learned the truth that comes from him, throw off your old sinful nature and your former way of life, which is corrupted by lust and deception. Instead, let the Spirit renew your thoughts and attitudes. Put on your new nature, created to be like God—truly righteous and holy" (Ephesians 4:21-24 NLT).

This is a two-part process. When we do our part, God does His. We are tasked with throwing off the old nature and the former way of life. When we do that, the Holy Spirit will renew our thoughts and attitudes and we are able to put on a new nature. So it's a cop-out for the believer to make the excuse of "I can't help myself." Help is available for the asking through God's Spirit when we yield to Him.

God can lead us to address the barriers in life in a way that reflects His righteousness and holiness. "Don't be conformed to the patterns of this world, but be transformed by the renewing of your minds so that you can figure out what God's will is—what is good and pleasing and mature" (Romans 12:2). If it were not possible for us to achieve it, God would not have instructed us to do so. He gives us the strength to fulfill His command: what God orders, He pays for.

The remedy for volume is self-control, which is the result of an authentic personal relationship with Jesus Christ. Time spent in prayer and simple silence before God, soaking up His love and becoming convinced of His desire for relationship with us, is powerful.

Take strength and instruction from James 1:19-22 (emphasis added): "Know this, my dear brothers and sisters: everyone should be quick to listen, slow to speak, and slow to grow angry. This is because an angry person doesn't produce God's righteousness. Therefore, with humility, set aside all moral filth and the growth of wickedness, and welcome the word planted deep inside you—the very word that is able to *save you.*"

If you are the one with the volume set at high, here are some tips that may help.

- **Understand what triggers you.** Ask yourself, *What situations push me over the edge? What topics, timing, or tactics from others push my buttons?* Discuss them with your mate for help to avoid playing into them.
- **Recognize the symptoms.** Do you feel tension in your body?

Do you find it difficult to listen just before the onslaught of words you later regret? Once you know the symptoms, you can consciously recognize when taking a time-out would be helpful.

- **Step away from the conversation.** Call a time-out to break the tension. Return to the conversation when you know you can manage the rushing tide of volume.
- **Recognize this is a spiritual issue with a biblical solution.** If it's become an issue you cannot manage without help, consider Christian counseling.

If you are the spouse married to one who often steps into the trap of volume, remember to use the four-step process to DEAL with it. It may sound something like this: "Yelling, shouting and screaming when you are upset or angry are not acceptable. I am not willing to tolerate these behaviors any longer. They always upset me and at times they frustrate or even frighten me. Trying to control these habits on your own has not been successful. I'm certain from what we've read in Scripture that this must grieve God, and it breaks my heart too. He has given you as a believer the strength and power through His Spirit to control your actions. As your mate, I ask you to do whatever it takes to gain and maintain control over this area of your communication. I love you and know that you are no happier with this situation than I am. How can I help you with this issue? I will support whatever you decide to do to address it, but it must be addressed. I believe we can become closer and more loving if you will tackle this behavior. What steps will you take?"

Remember you cannot control your spouse's behavior or manage his or her actions. This conversation may be very uncomfortable for you and you might be concerned it will turn up the volume in response. If it does, remember to let your spouse know that you are serious about not accepting this form of communication and step away from the conversation. Be clear that you are eager to return to the discussion once the volume comes down and then suggest a time-out.

Pray for your mate and allow the Spirit of God to build your faith in this situation. Meditate on the Scriptures found in the resource section of this chapter.

It's difficult when your mate's volume increases to the point you feel you must match it in order to make yourself heard. Resist the temptation. Offer mercy where it's undeserved, grace when retaliation seems instinctive. "A gentle answer deflects anger, but harsh words make tempers flare" (Proverbs 15:1 NLT). Your generous response may startle your mate into recognizing the disparity between your self-control and the lack of control he or she is expressing. Your godly example may be the lifeline God uses in the moment.

Silence, sulking, sarcasm, and sound: these are the barriers to the life God longs for us to know as His sons and daughters. We can achieve the level of connection and intimacy we hoped for the day we wed. It's possible when we stand on the Word of God and yield to His Spirit to lead and guide us into all truth.

When we stand, *fighting together as one flesh,* against the enemy, we break through these barriers and reflect the life Christ died to secure for us. Our marriages glorify Him as we reflect the character of the King in this life.

Let's put on the gloves and demolish these barriers and begin living the life that comes when we follow Him.

Put on the Gloves! Chapter 6

If possible, we recommend both spouses complete this entire section. Respond to the questions individually, and then come together for a discussion. If you are completing this process alone, record your thoughts to the questions and use the conversation starters for a discussion with your spouse. Record what each of you shares in the "He said / She said" section.

1. Which traps are you most likely to indulge in? How do they present? What damaging impact results from the behavior?

2. What steps can you take to break through these barriers? What Scriptures from this chapter will give you the hope and direction you will need to follow through?

He Said / She Said

Use these questions to build a discussion with your spouse. Then each enter your thoughts in a "He Said / She Said" section of your journal.

- How would our relationship be different if we could eliminate these barriers? Be specific.
- How can we become more consistent in dealing with them? What steps of DEAL will be most helpful?
- What permissions will we give each other to address these behaviors when they occur?

God Said

"What is the source of conflict among you? What is the source of your disputes? Don't they come from your cravings that are at war in your own lives? You long for something you don't have, so you commit murder. You are jealous for something you can't get, so you struggle and fight. You don't have because you don't ask. You ask and don't have because you ask with evil intentions, to waste it on your own cravings" (James 4:1-3).

What is the source of your conflict? What "cravings" are at war in your lives? What's the impact of those issues that you now recognize and are ready to demolish?

NEW DISCOVERIES / HOW CAN WE USE THIS INFORMATION?

Be specific! Write in your journal what stands out to you from this chapter.

PRAYER

Thank you, Lord, for your Word and your Spirit who guides us into all truth. We stand together ready to break through the barriers that have held us back. We call on you, Lord, to strengthen us for the work ahead to eliminate the traps that have tripped us up. Thank you that through you we can do all things in Christ Jesus, abolishing the old habits of our former selves and surrendering to the work you desire to do in each of us. Help us walk in the knowledge of our new life as new creatures, made to reflect your character in this life. Thank you for your gifts of grace, mercy, and patience; may we invest them in each other as you have done in us. We love you, Lord, and praise you for the promise of unity in you and with you.

CHAPTER 7

YOUR PAST DOESN'T HAVE TO BE YOUR FUTURE

"We have history together."

That statement might be one of victory—acknowledgment that our years of shared experience have built a solid foundation and we are deeper in love than we were the day we married.

On the other hand, the same statement can be an expression of animosity and antagonism, evidenced by the years of discord we've spent as husband and wife.

Even when we are deeply committed to life in Christ and are open to learning new tools and approaches to make our marriage successful, our *history together* can sometimes be a problem. Though situations come and go, we still have memories of times when our life as a couple created pain, disappointment, and frustration. How do we avoid the temptation to resurrect the old hurts and avoid carrying them into today? How do we ignore what feels like familiar territory and dismiss the *Here we go again* thoughts and feelings?

Failing to fully forgive past hurts and fighting to forget the painful shared history will undermine even the most skilled couple. This chapter explores biblical strategies and tools to move beyond this barrier.

This obstacle can feel insurmountable, so let's begin by understanding the foundations for marriage itself: the concept of covenant.

Covenant Versus Contract

What is a *covenant*? In essence, a covenant is an agreement between two parties, established by a joint commitment before God as their witness. It's an agreement intended to be permanent, binding the parties together, and is protected by God.

The day Ron and I stood at the altar, we created a covenant as we entered into marriage, becoming husband and wife. We stood before witnesses, including God, to declare our commitment. Because it is ultimately *God* who has joined us as marriage partners together, we vowed ourselves to each other "'til death do us part." That's a forever promise.

Matthew 19:6 reinforces the permanence of marriage: "So they are no longer two but one flesh." Many translations use the word *cleave* as God directs husband and wife to join their lives and leave mother and father behind. It's an interesting word. In his commentary on Genesis: 2:24, Bill Lawrence shares this insight on the process: "The concept of *cleave* portrays a vivid picture. It describes *glue*. When we marry we are stuck *to* (not *with*) each other.

For glue to work, there must be pressure applied to the joint where the two elements are joined together." In other words, pressure applied creates a tighter, more secure bond. The pressure may come from conflict, disappointment, hurt, or a myriad of other possibilities.

While the pain of the pressure may be intense, it serves a purpose: it helps to cement the bond between husband and wife.

"Therefore, humans must not pull apart what God has put together" (Mark 10:9). No one. *Not even the couple themselves.* We often read this as a warning to outsiders not to interfere with the marriage, which is true. But more often, the assault on the covenant comes from within, made by either husband or wife or both.

It's important to remember when a Christ-following couple enters into the marriage covenant, there are three persons involved: a husband, a wife, and God. It's God's Word that governs the marriage relationship as the couple commits to conduct their lives according to God's design and plan. God's plan is "as long as you both shall live."

Many couples come to the altar with Plan B already in mind. Marriage has become less a lifetime covenant and more a contract that can be amended ("We have an open marriage by mutual agreement") or dissolved ("I deserve to be happy and you don't make me happy").

Covenant versus contract: let's examine the qualities and characteristics of these two agreements. Note on which side of the scale you find your relationship.

Covenant	Contract
Actively participates in the relationship to ensure growth and development.	Participates in the relationship as needed to maintain or achieve short-term goals, or to avoid unpleasantness.
Commits consistently at high levels to sustain connection, agreement with spouse, and alignment with God's Word.	Commits to specific, stated requirements for level of response desired.
Collaborative—flexible in sharing duties and responsibilities. Does what needs doing to support the relationship.	Prefers clearly defined roles and responsibilities. Does only what is required to fulfill his or her obligation.
High levels of trust in his or her mate based on shared values and joint commitment to live according to the Scriptures.	Contract driven: "If you, then I..." Trust is placed in the contract or agreement, not in the person.
Solves problems through collaboration; focuses on solutions that provide mutual benefit.	Positional problem solving; campaigns for solution most personally beneficial.
Works through conflict as a partner, not an adversary. Looks for win / win solutions.	Drives for concessions and personal agenda; uses position power.
Communicates openly and consistently to ensure understanding and agreement.	Limited and sometimes formal communication.

Accepts risk as a shared responsibility with spouse.	Limits risk for oneself. Absolves self of risk not specifically assigned to him or her.
Shares information freely—open and transparent. Views shared information as vital to relationship.	Limits shared information; works on a need-to-know basis. Views information as power.

The two are very different. There is no evidence of the "two becoming one" under a contractual agreement. It's more of an "every man for himself" existence, similar to roommates, that if found to be inconvenient can be disposed of quickly.

Law Versus Love

We can connect the concept of covenant to love: love of spouse and love for God. In the same manner, we can make a correlation between a contract and the law; contracts are only viable and enforceable under the law. Let's review these two further, by comparing and contrasting their characteristics.

Law	Love
The law is black and white, inflexible, focused on minute details.	Love overlooks, forgives, and grants pardon.
The law is conditional: "If you, then I…"	Love is unconditional.

The law seeks to benefit itself. Its only fulfillment is to be obeyed.	Love is fulfilled when it is given away.
The law is without emotion and without mercy, and it pronounces judgment.	Love is full of mercy and suspends judgment.
The law demands a high price to be paid if it is not observed correctly.	Love pays the price.
The law is designed to rule by power; it enforces norms and standards of behavior.	Love is easily satisfied and does not demand on behalf of self.

If a marriage is ruled by contract or law, it leaves a lot to be desired, doesn't it? The law is inflexible and coercive, enforcing standards established through harsh penalty. It creates relationship based on the conditional proposition that *If you do as I require, then I will not punish you, or I may even provide you with some benefit.* Wasn't that the arrangement between God and man after the fall in the garden and before the death of Christ on our behalf?

Before grace, relationship between God and man was built on the law given to Moses. The book of Leviticus provides a thorough and detailed description of the requirements by which man could maintain relationship with God under the law. There was a lot of blood involved. It required daily attention and a constant investment of time. The next required act of obedience was never far from one's mind, because the penalties for failing to follow the law were substantial.

Sounds like some marriages. Plagued by demand and obedience, inflexible and insisting on personal preference, these relationships choke out the potential for intimacy, unity, and alignment with each other and God. Grudges are nursed like babies at the breast. Walls are erected, bridges are burned, and the structure of the marriage divides like the waters of the Red Sea.

But love is quite another matter. There's an element of promise, hope, and possibility in a relationship rooted and grounded in love.

Love accomplishes what the law cannot. And love is a choice. Even when your unhappy history together threatens the potential for success, your past need not define your future, but it will if you allow it to do so.

Forgiveness Is Not Optional

God makes a choice about the sins of our past. He casts them into the sea of forgetfulness, never to remember them against us. His choice is motivated by love. Unlike God, we may never forget. Short of a serious head injury or amnesia, our souls (minds) can call up the pain like high-speed video on demand. If we allow it to play, we'll be transported back in time to when the offense, the lie, or the broken trust occurred, with all of the accompanying emotion it brought in that moment.

Replaying that movie is dangerous and it's a symptom of a treacherous, contractual way of thinking and living. Why is this dangerous?

- Those reruns tempt us to bring the hurt to the table once again and present them as evidence in the here and now.
- We expect to see the behavior or action repeat, and we leap on the slightest hint of a recurrence, even though the offending partner asked forgiveness and received it.

- And in the worst scenario, the breach in the relationship has never been forgiven nor has it been forgotten. The injured party waits for the opportunity to return the hurt "so you can see how it feels. Mark my words, I'm not going to forget this anytime soon."

Unless this is a commitment to always remember how wonderful the spouse is or how much his or her act of kind generosity is appreciated, this statement is not usually a predictor of good things to come. "I'll be back," Arnold Schwarzenegger's famous line from the movie *Terminator,* was not a promise. It was a threat.

Settling the Score Is a Losing Game

Payback. Retribution. Vengeance. All are words to define vindictiveness. A full description rattles the bones: *Having or showing a desire to hurt someone who has hurt or caused problems for you. Spiteful. Inclined to revenge or retaliation.* It's never going to sit well with God as it's the *law* in full operation—punishment, tit for tat, gotcha! He has a lot to say on the subject.

Vindication is about keeping score with the full intent to settle it in the future; battle lines are drawn. The goal is to give what you got or perhaps a bit worse than what you got. There's an element of *You may have gotten the best of me this time, but payback will be miserable. I'd watch out if I were you.*

Hardly sounds like romantic pillow talk, does it? Couples who fall into this pattern sound more like sworn enemies than lovers. Let's not forget who the real enemy is: "For we are not fighting against flesh-and-blood enemies, but against evil rulers and authorities of the unseen world, against mighty powers in this dark world, and against evil spirits in the heavenly places" (Ephesians 6:12 NLT). The enemy's strategy is twofold:

- First, as we wait for just the right time to unleash the upset, he tickles our ear with whispered accusations against our covenant partner, whipping up the emotions of the past.
- Second, once we're thoroughly prepared, he inspires us to turn on each other while he stands by and enjoys the spectacle as we attack and our unity comes unglued.

Remember the wife who stayed silent for nearly twenty years, then announced she wanted a divorce? She'd been entertaining the whispered indictments a very long time before she took her revenge and settled the score. Having the final say may have been satisfying, but she lived through a lot of unhappiness to get there.

We are robbed of our logic, our common sense, and our spiritual maturity when we settle on vindictiveness as a method to deal with conflict or upset.

Marriages were envisioned and created by God to unite two into one, to emulate the relationship of Christ and the church. The Bible has much to say on this topic of revenge.

- "Never pay back evil with more evil. Do things in such a way that everyone can see you are honorable" (Romans 12:17 NLT).
- "Don't pay back evil for evil or insult for insult. Instead, give blessing in return. You were called to do this so that you might inherit a blessing" (1 Peter 3:9).

- "Don't say, 'I'll do to them what they did to me. I'll pay them back for their actions'" (Proverbs 24:29).

"But you don't know what he said!" "You have no idea how badly she hurt me!" You may be right, and perhaps no one understands it. No one but Jesus: "When they hurled their insults at him, he did not retaliate; when he suffered, he made no threats. Instead, he entrusted himself to him who judges justly" (1 Peter 2:23 NIV). Even then Jesus operated in love.

He is our example. How can we expect that of ourselves or each other? He was the Son of God, the Messiah, and the long awaited Savior! How can we possibly measure up? He was fully God and fully man, tempted in every way that we will encounter. He certainly had both the reason and the power to retaliate. Yet He chose not to do so. We can make that same choice.

Christ chose to love us when we were anything but lovable. He knew every last secret, every shred of pride and rebellion, every ugly thought. All of it. He loved us still. And He asks us to do the same.

Love Is Required

Demonstrating love on a daily basis is not easy. Some people are hard to love. They are difficult, arrogant, opinionated, prideful, selfish, and the list goes on. It does not matter to Christ. To love those who are lovable is nothing special—even those who walk without Jesus can manage that. He asks us to love those whose behavior is hurtful and damaging.

> You have heard that it was said, "You shall love your neighbor and hate your enemy." But I say to you, love your enemies, bless those

who curse you, do good to those who hate you, and pray for those who spitefully use you and persecute you, that you may be sons of your Father in heaven; for He makes His sun rise on the evil and on the good, and sends rain on the just and on the unjust. For if you love those who love you, what reward have you? Do not even the tax collectors do the same? And if you greet your brethren only, what do you do more than others? Do not even the tax collectors do so? (Matthew. 5:43-47 NKJV)

That's a tall order. Being civil is not sufficient. Love those who seem determined to take you down, to hurt and demean you. Pray for the ones who use you in a spiteful way. Remember that before we trusted in Christ, we were just as unlovely in the eyes of a perfect and spotless Lord Jesus. If we can't or won't make this our goal, we are failing to follow the foundations of life in Christ.

Love defines our lives as Christians and should be the backbone of our marriages and every interaction we have. We are instructed to model our love for each other after the love God has shown us. Love seeks to benefit others at the expense of itself. The law demands to be satisfied at the expense of others.

How is it possible? We are made new in Him. We are not fixed-up versions of our former selves but new creations. It's not easy, but it's possible, as we grow in the reality of the completed work at the cross.

We've been given this powerful choice to pass forgiveness along. First Corinthians 13:5 says, "[Love] doesn't keep a record of complaints." No record, no retaliation. "Be tolerant with each other and, if someone has a complaint against anyone, forgive each other. As the Lord forgave you, so also forgive each other" (Colossians 3:13).

Making the choice to let go of past hurt, betrayal, or anger is possible only through love. This is the work of the Holy Spirit in our lives. Refuse to partner with the enemy. Rejecting his whispered accusations requires vigilance; he seizes every opportunity, but he cannot compete with love. "Therefore, submit to God. Resist the devil, and he will run away from you. Come near to God, and he will come near to you" (James 4:7-8).

On occasion most of us fight to forgive and fail to forget. The Scriptures provide all the insights and tips needed to take down this barrier. Meditate on the Bible verses in this section and ask God to strengthen you and free you from the trap of vindictiveness. All parties are damaged when it's in play.

Revenge is an old, old trap. Even in the 1600s in a sermon titled "Apples of Sodom," British clergyman Jeremy Taylor said that revenge "is like a rolling stone, which, when a man hath forced up a hill, will return upon him with a greater violence, and break those bones whose sinews gave it motion."

So let's put on the gloves and fight to establish, protect, and serve our covenant!

Put on the Gloves! Chapter 7

If possible, we recommend both spouses complete this entire section. Respond to the questions individually, and then come together for a discussion. If you are completing this process alone, record your thoughts to the questions and use the conversation starters for a discussion with your spouse. Record what each of you shares in the "He said / She said" section.

1. As you consider the difference between love and law, covenant and contract, where would you place your marriage at present? What are the signs? What evidence can you identify for your assessment?

2. How much of an issue is unforgiveness, retaliation, or revenge in your relationship? What discoveries came through this chapter, and what impact did they have on you?

He Said / She Said

Use these questions to build a discussion with your spouse. Then each enter your thoughts in a "He Said / She Said" section of your journal.

- How would our relationship be better if we could fully forgive and move forward without resurrecting old hurts? Be specific.
- How can we establish our covenant and leave the contracts behind? What can we do to walk together in love and leave the curse of the law behind?

God Said

Read this passage of Scripture and discuss.

"Therefore, humans must not pull apart what God has put together" (Mark 10:9).

Read this quote and discuss its meaning.

"In taking revenge, a man is but even with his enemy; but in passing it over, he is superior." —Francis Bacon

Who is the true enemy of your marriage covenant? How can you join forces against him?

New Discoveries / How Can We Use This Information?

Be specific! Write in your journal what stands out to you from this chapter.

Prayer

Lord, thank you for the covenant of marriage. You established it, you witnessed it, and you expect us to be good caretakers of the gift that comes through it. We cancel any contracts we've entered into together and commit to honoring and protecting our marriage covenant. Help us recognize that pressure applied will strengthen our bond, and we give your Spirit full permission to remind us in difficult moments of your presence in the process. Because we have been fully forgiven, teach us to forgive each other fully. We declare we will no longer entertain the enemy's whispered accusations against each other and will resist him until he flees, as your Word declares. Thank you for helping us walk fully as one in you.

CHAPTER 8

RULES OF ENGAGEMENT: LEARNING TO FIGHT FAIR

We had agreed before church that we'd leave as soon as Ron's Saturday evening service responsibilities were complete. The afternoon had been filled with family activity and we had skipped lunch. We were both exhausted and hungry. Home and dinner were the goals for the evening.

At the conclusion of service, Ron shot out of the pew in time to speak with someone about the men's ministry meeting for the following evening. When I glanced in that direction a few moments later, he was gone. I looked around the sanctuary but couldn't spot him. *And they say women are the talkers. They don't know Ron.*

I was annoyed but moved toward the foyer hoping he might be waiting for me there. No luck. I asked several friends, but no one remembered seeing him after the close of service. I walked the building but couldn't find him. Now I was beginning to move from annoyed to irritated. It was a fairly short trip. Fatigue and an empty stomach egged me on. It's my only excuse.

Finally, I called him on his cell phone. No answer, but within a moment or two he emerged from a small side room off the sanctuary. He looked around and caught my eye but didn't join me at the back of the church. He hitched his thumb over his right shoulder. *Sorry, I don't read sign language.* I walked slowly toward him.

"I have to count the offering, babe." Not news. He does it every week. But the social butterfly he'd been impersonating delayed that significantly. It had been nearly twenty-five minutes since the final prayer. I'd spent fifteen of those looking for him.

"Are you almost done?"

He shook his head. "Just got started." I glared. He assured me he'd be done as quickly as possible and returned to the office. I stood, stewing, staring at the closed door.

I went to the foyer and found a place to sit.

The battle lines had been drawn. I was ready for a showdown. Or maybe it was a meltdown, I can't recall, but whichever it was—*it was on.*

The Showdown and the Lesson

When Ron exited the office he headed straight to where I was seated. "Ready?"

It was all I could do to nod politely. But the gloves came off when we got in the car. Oh, he was apologetic and immediately suggested we have dinner out rather than go home to cook. That made me madder. We'd been working hard to save money, and limiting restaurant meals was one of the commitments we'd made. So that sent me down an entirely new path. I reminded him that this always seemed to happen and he never thought about the impact on me when it did. I easily came up with at least three similar infractions and shared them in great detail. I let him know that I was not feeling well now, and I was certain it was because I hadn't eaten, thank you very much.

I'll spare you the remaining detail, but it's fair to say that when it was all over, there was a lot of apologizing and accepting responsibility for bad behavior.

And that was from me.

In less than five minutes, I managed to break at least four of our rules for dealing with conflict. If you're going to fight, you have to fight fair. I hadn't stuck to that plan and I needed to own it. Ugh. I know I'm not always going to be right, but I hate it when I'm wrong. The Holy Spirit tapped on my heart and quietly said, "Put a fork in it. It's done."

So to heap hot coals on my head, when we arrived home, Ron sent me to change into something more comfortable (and perhaps someone more likable) and made dinner while I relaxed. *Could he be any more annoying?*

For a girl who grew up without conflict in her home, I've sure adapted well.

In fairness, it also works the other way around at our house. We trade the roles back and forth quite evenly. It doesn't last long, but when we ignore the boundaries, we pay the price.

Boundaries Keep You Safe

Boundaries establish acceptable behavior in marriage and define what will not be tolerated in the relationship. And if it's not acceptable to God, it's out-of-bounds, no matter what the two of you might be willing to accept.

God's Word establishes many boundaries for husband and wife, but we are also subject to those He sets for how we deal with the brethren. It's easy to forget we play dual roles in each other's life: husband and wife, as well as brother and sister in Christ.

God gave Moses the Ten Commandments, which are often thought of as *The Big Rules*. If it's been a while, read them over. They're designed to protect us and keep us from harm or pain or loss. God created them for *our* benefit.

Some may chafe at the idea of rules between husband and wife. Others don't like the concept of rules at all. Call them *guidelines* or *agreements* if you are more comfortable with those words. They all have the same function: to help us fight *together* when the enemy takes aim at our marriage.

The rules may help us avoid conflict altogether at times. So the agreements we establish as husband and wife are designed to serve us, to support the marriage, and to glorify God in the process. And when conflict does hunt us down, the rules guide us to fight fair and use our differences to strengthen us, not tear us apart.

"We demolish arguments and every pretension that sets itself up against the knowledge of God, and we take captive every thought to make it obedient to Christ" (2 Corinthians 10:5 NIV). Demolish, annihilate, eliminate, defeat, or crush arguments. Sound good?

OK, so if God's Word has it covered, why make rules? Won't they be dismissed or forgotten in the heat of the battle? They can be. But when you have established agreements, guidelines created together and agreed upon, you have common ground on which to address the out-of-bounds behavior in a way your spouse cannot dismiss.

You each have ownership, since you created the rules together. And we protect the things we own. It's important to remember the rules aren't handcuffs to lock down your mate. They're handrails to steady you both when the discussion gets off track.

As we said in the first chapter, no one hands you a set of rules when you marry. For us, they emerged over time, often after a particularly difficult conflict. The agreements may be slightly different for each couple. Use our list as seed-thoughts to customize your own rules so they work for your marriage, based on your particular personalities and baggage.

It's important to reinforce that much of what's been covered in previous chapters include important guidelines, so we did not add them here. If a topic or tool deserved a chapter of its own, consider it vital. Respect is not listed because it's multifaceted. It is *represented* throughout the set. If you are surprised not to see it listed by itself, it's purposeful. We've included the *behaviors* that describe *how to respect,* rather than saying, "Respect each other."

So here are the types of rules we've found helpful over the years. They are organized to support you at each step of the interaction:

- Foundational: Before an issue arises
- Approach: As you enter the discussion
- Discover: Explore and discuss
- Challenges: In the heat of the moment
- Back on Track: When the dust settles

To build a house that will stand through good times and bad, you need a strong foundation. Let's start at the very beginning—the foundational agreements—that can change the trajectory of your conflict and your life.

THE FOUR FOUNDATIONAL AGREEMENTS:
BEFORE AN ISSUE ARISES

This first set of rules will place your marriage on solid footing. These are primary tenets of faith essential in the marital relationship. God expects us to honor them, regardless of the difference of opinion that may be simmering. We call them foundational because, without them, life is a melee in the making where anything goes. All bets are off. These are the basics, which must be discussed and agreed on as defining how you live as marrieds. They address a wide spectrum of how you do life together as followers of Jesus. Establish them during peacetime, so when conflict arises you're prepared to deal with it constructively and positioned to avoid damage. The outcome is a solution that makes you both happy.

Let's review the foundations.

1. *The Word of God is the blueprint for your life as believers.* "Every scripture is inspired by God and is useful for teaching, for showing mistakes, for correcting, and for training character" (2 Timothy 3:16).

When husband and wife agree that God's Word will be the *final word* in their lives, life is good. I may prefer one solution and Ron another. But we benefit by consulting the Bible to see what God has to say on the topic. Scripture provides the foundation for alignment with God and with each other. Accept God's Word as the first and foundational rule. Consider these verses:

- "The people who love your Instruction enjoy peace—and lots of it. There's no stumbling for them!" (Psalm 119:165).

- "My people are destroyed from lack of knowledge. Since you have rejected knowledge, so I will reject you from serving me as a priest. Since you have forgotten the Instruction of your God, so also I will forget your children" (Hosea 4:6).

Knowledge is obtainable through the Scriptures, and the Holy Spirit will lead us into full understanding. Knowledge applied in the moment needed is called *wisdom*. Wisdom doesn't get itself wrapped up in a knot during conflict. Wisdom keeps a clear head and is focused on doing what is pleasing to God.

2. *Don't fight in front of the kids.* If the conflict starts in the presence of your children, defer it to a time you can address it without an audience or move to another space where you can discuss it privately. Children are hapless bystanders and can become emotional or fearful quickly. Additionally, they may find it difficult to forget the words they heard long after the two of you have kissed and made up.

3. *Don't use the D word.* Invoking the word *divorce* is the ultimate threat and it's electrifying; it accelerates the blaze like gas on a fire. It's an affront to a covenant relationship and the one who witnessed it—God. It's rarely anything beyond an attention-grabber meant to twist the knife. It often comes from the person who thinks he or she is losing the argument as a way to shock the other and gain the upper hand. Don't go there.

4. *Exclude violence.* Violence is off the table from the get-go. Physicality changes the dynamic of a relationship, instilling fear in the injured party. Violence doesn't always result in physical injury. Pushing, raising a hand as if to strike, even menacingly standing over someone is intimidating and destructive behavior that must never be accepted. Even the threat of violence can eliminate or reduce

intimacy and replace it with the need to self-protect. If this is a pattern you or your spouse has been unable to break, it may be time to seek outside counseling and support.

Those are the big four foundational rules. Consider them sacred and honor them. You will see an immediate improvement in your ability to deal with conflict successfully.

The next group of rules helps us get started on the right foot when our differences must be addressed.

APPROACH: As You Enter the Discussion

The only thing that counts is where you finish. *Not.* We disagree 100 percent with this mind-set. How you *start* is how you finish. Come out swinging and the fight is off and running. Pounce on your spouse with friends along for the ride at Friday's dinner and a show—and plan to walk home.

The finish is often *determined* by the approach. Take time to consider questions like: *How can I create the best atmosphere possible so we can have a productive discussion? What's the best way to approach this to avoid hurt and ugliness? What can we do to create a solution we're both happy with?* Don't step into the ring without preparing yourself. It's a quick way to blow it up before you ever get started.

You can do this. And there are rules to help.

1. *Pray.* Before you discuss a topic that may be difficult, pray. Perhaps you recognize an issue that needs to be addressed, but your spouse is unaware. Pray for God to go before you and prepare your mate's heart. Petition God for the right words to introduce the topic and ask for self-control if needed. Be sensitive about when to initiate the conversation and seek God's direction for timing. (This is addressed in the next rule.)

If you and your spouse have defined the topic and come to discuss it, pray together before you begin. Ask God to be present in the process and confirm your commitment together that you will yield to His voice. Express your desire to honor each other in the conversation and for peace to serve as the umpire (read Colossians 3:15 in The Amplified Bible). Declare your commitment to fighting fair. See the resource section in the back of this book for a sample declaration.

2. *Timing is everything.* Refer to the *S* in SPEAK, our communication tool: *Seek* permission to have the conversation now. The fact that you're ready to discuss it doesn't mean your spouse is. Pay attention. Is Friday night at the airport after your wife's long road trip a good time to hit her up with an issue you've been stewing about all week? If you're hoping your husband will agree to spend the holidays with your family instead of his this year, do you think the night before his big presentation is the best time to bring it up?

Springing a big topic on your spouse without considering the timing can feel like a surprise attack. If that's your plan, don't expect your mate to participate productively. He or she may accommodate you in the moment with a half-hearted, "Yeah, okay. If that's what you want, I guess it's okay." Or he or she may respond to the attack with aggression and reject the idea without any genuine consideration. Neither of those is a good outcome.

Consider the timing and seek permission for the discussion. Get this one right and you set yourself up for a great interaction with the potential to fix, change, create, solve, or produce something wonderful. Get it wrong and prepare for disappointment. Choose wisely.

When partners are involved in conflict, partnership is required to achieve a peaceful outcome. This next rule reminds us—it takes two.

3. *Both partners will actively work toward peace.* "If it is possible, as far as it depends on you, live at peace with everyone" (Romans 12:18 NIV). This verse from Romans makes it clear that peace is God's desire and expectation. It also seems to acknowledge it may not always be easy. The words "as it depends on you" are important. They are related to the final element in DEAL, our tool for facing conflict. *L* stands for *Let go of the need to manage your mate's behavior. Manage your own.* In other words, each person is responsible for managing his or her conduct in the conversation. Silent treatment, sulking, sarcasm, and sound (volume and tone) are choices to avoid—that's a major part of self-management. Dodging the temptation of these behaviors is key to pursuing peace, and the only way to achieve it is to work together.

James is bold in his description of the power of the tongue: "And among all the parts of the body, the tongue is a flame of fire. It is a whole world of wickedness, corrupting your entire body. It can set your whole life on fire, for it is set on fire by hell itself" (3:6 NLT). *The power to set your whole life on fire.*

There is an old cliché that says, "You can be right or you can be happy." It's overused because it's true. When you insist on your own way at all costs, you create an adversarial environment. Wringing the last bit of concession out of your mate while refusing to listen to other possible solutions will suck the life out of your marriage. If there's a winner, there's a loser. Do you want to be married to a loser? *I didn't think so.* It's simple to fix: don't force your spouse into that role. You may win this round and lose the match. Your goal is win / win.

When there is a difference of opinion, thought, belief, or approach—the potential for conflict exists. Where it goes from there and whether it ends with peace, or not, depends on you. Here are the possibilities.

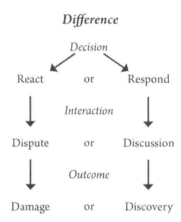

Difference

Decision

React   or   Respond

Interaction

Dispute   or   Discussion

Outcome

Damage   or   Discovery

Which path you travel is your decision. But when you have agreed in advance that peace will be your focus, you have a good chance to get there together. A commitment to peace is a noble goal and one God will bless. The Holy Spirit stands at the ready to intercede with a reminder to soften the tone or choose your words wisely as emotions rise. An open discussion, where you are willing to hear what your loved one thinks and says, is worth the effort. And it has the best chance of producing a solution that works.

Managing your mouth is a big step toward operating in peace. There are additional rules about what you say and how you say it as you approach the discussion. Let's take a look at some guidelines that help you start strong.

4. *If it's not a big deal, don't make it a big deal.* Differentiate the petty annoyances from the deal breakers. I might prefer Chinese food and Ron's been thinking Italian. Is it worth a throw down? Or a

meltdown? No. The huff I worked myself into after church was silly and selfish. Wasted energy. In the moment, the enemy whispers and we become convinced by our fatigue or hunger or frustration that we've been wronged and we're tempted to go all in. Remember who the tempter is! Toilet seats left up, lights left on, dirty dishes crusting in the sink: none of these warrant the energy (or potential discord) of a conflict. Make your request, but save yourself the unnecessary emotion. "I just feel disrespected when he leaves the toilet seat up." Oh, get over it. It's carelessness, not disrespect. One's accidental, the other is purposeful. Don't turn it into something it's not.

One of the qualities I (Deb) admired most about my mother was her ability to let things go. If someone cut her off in traffic she'd say, "Must be going someplace important." And there was no snarkasm there. She meant it. If my dad said something careless, she'd smile at him and he got the message. At some point in life, she made a decision to give others, even strangers, the benefit of the doubt. She refused to pick up the offense or let small things loom large in her life. She didn't live in a bubble; she was aware of the snub or unkind remark, but she was undisturbed by it. Ron once said to me, "They say you can tell what a woman will be like as she ages by observing her mother." He looked across the table at me. "I'm still waiting. All I see is your dad." It was not a compliment. *I'm working on it.*

"A person's wisdom yields patience; it is to one's glory to overlook an offense" (Proverbs 19:11 NIV). Choose not to be offended over insignificant matters. Life hands us enough big stuff without our manufacturing extra drama.

5. *Touch.* Physical touch connects us. As you begin your discussion, be purposeful about that connection. Hold hands across the

kitchen table. Sit next to each other on the couch. It's a statement: *We're on the same side. We're not adversaries. We're in this together.*

So let's review where you are. You've established the foundational rules that set you up for success. You've also been intentional about how and when to approach your spouse about the topic. Great job! You're on your way.

Now the heavy lifting begins. It's time to engage each other to explore the subject at hand. Skill power, including SPEAK and DEAL, will help you in addition to the rules in the next section.

DISCOVER: EXPLORE AND DISCUSS

No clairvoyance allowed. Your spouse can't read your mind and you can't read his or hers. The assumptions we make lead to assigning a motive: "I know exactly what you're thinking—that I'm selfish." We then respond as though the person actually said, "You're selfish." It's not accurate or fair. And any response to our mind-reading game is based on a lie.

It is possible your assumption of your mate's thought is accurate, but he or she gets credit for not tossing it around. Resist the urge to put words in the mouth of your loved one. Clarifying works better than clairvoyance. It's next on our list.

"What did you say?" In the heat of the moment we don't always listen fully. We often think ahead, hearing what we *believe* was said. Before you respond, verify you heard correctly. Paraphrase your understanding of what your spouse said and ask for a confirmation (or clarification) so you are on the same page. It's a quick summary of what you heard and understood and concludes with a closed-ended question. It sounds like this: "So from what you're describing, it sounds like you think I'm being selfish. Is that how you feel?"

The response will either confirm your statement or clarify and correct it. Either way, you now have shared understanding and that helps you take the next steps together.

Clean up after yourself. Take responsibility for your part of the mess. Were you rude or inconsiderate? Own it. Did you break a trust or disregard a commitment? Acknowledge it. Nothing stops the momentum of ugliness as much as the statement, "I was wrong. I'm so sorry."

Collaborate. Brainstorming is a creative process. Use it to consider possible options and discover an answer together. To do this effectively, let the ideas flow without stopping to judge each one. Duck the urge to throw cold water on a suggestion with a quick "Oh that won't work." Write them *all* down. Create as many as possible, no matter how crazy an idea might seem. Once you've got a healthy list, go back and review them together. What can you quickly eliminate because of expense or time available? Cross them off. Is there one you both like, but it doesn't fully address the issue? Consider combining it with one of the other ideas that will fill in the gap.

Keep working at it until you find something you can both support that meets the need, solves the problem, or resolves the conflict. The best ideas are often a mash-up of what your spouse suggests added to a thought you have and—voilà! You have a custom-built solution.

Stay on track. Define the topic and stick to it. If additional issues come up, acknowledge them and set them aside to deal with at a later time. This will allow you to focus on the immediate need. Give each other permission to identify when you have wandered, and both make a commitment to keep your attention on the matter at hand.

Stay out of the weeds. "You said I was twenty minutes late. You're wrong. I was only fourteen minutes late." You were late. Don't get lost in the minutiae. When you pick apart every word or debate over little details, you lose your way on the path to peace. A GPS for couple's conflict would be great: "Return to the route" would be helpful in the moment. Lacking that, you will need to manage this detour on your own.

Lighten up! Take the discussion seriously but yourself less so. Countless times in the middle of a conflict Ron and I have burst into laughter over how serious we've become over something inconsequential. Laughter creates connection and it's healing. Don't stifle it. A good laugh is good for the soul.

Warning! Done poorly, this can backfire. Laugh together, not at each other.

Challenges: In the Heat of the Moment

We've established guidelines for a positive, productive discussion. Despite our best intentions, we may allow emotion to rule our behavior or escalate the situation. When the heat goes up, the rules are there to serve you. Let's review them.

Avoid the absolutes. When used in an accusation, "Always" and "never" are almost always inaccurate! It allows the prosecutor in each of us to react, saying, "Oh, yes I did! Remember that one time seven years ago on vacation? I seem to recall…" Be genuine as you lay out your concern and don't overstate your case by invoking the absolutes. No one's on trial here—or at least no one should be. This approach rarely has the desired effect and often creates a rebuttal. It's not helpful.

Don't interrupt. An interruption says, "What I have to say is more important, so you can stop talking now." Just don't. Use a notepad to take notes while your spouse is speaking to capture anything you'd like to respond to. Wait your turn; it helps you avoid a reaction and form a response instead. If you want to reap respect in the conversation, sow respect.

Don't make threats. A threat is a promise of something unpleasant, damaging, or hurtful. It prophesies retaliation, revenge, or punishment, which we covered in earlier chapters. Regardless of whether the threat is physical or emotional, it must be off-limits. It's evidence of a contract, not a covenant. A contract is all about conditions. Love is unconditional. Focus on love, not law.

Eventually, we do find our way out of the chaos. The light at the end of the tunnel appears and we're almost certain it's not an oncoming train. A lot of back and forth has gone on and there may be some bruised hearts or battered pride. What now? Let's take a look at getting back on track.

Back on Track: When the Dust Settles

Pray together. Offer forgiveness to your spouse and ask for it as well. Ask God to forgive you as a couple for grieving Him and disrespecting the covenant. Remind each other of your love and confirm your commitment to walking together in a God-honoring relationship. Acknowledge your need for His direction to implement the steps you've agreed on.

Hold each other. If it's been loud and ugly, you may feel as though you've survived a car wreck together. Reconnect emotionally and physically before you move on.

Here are some practical next-steps to build some momentum and healing.

Debrief. Discussing the discussion after it's over is called a *debriefing*. The purpose of a debriefing is to understand how your behavior impacted the outcome. When you've had a dust-up and fought through to restore the peace, learn from it! The goal is to make new mistakes—avoiding the repetitive patterns that trap us. You also want to celebrate and understand the positive steps and patterns that worked.

Did you create a productive process leading to discovery? Identify how you accomplished that so you can do it again. Or did your actions create discord that ended in damage, even if you did finally reach agreement? Discuss where the conversation ran off the rails and took you someplace you didn't want to go. This equips you to avoid it in the future.

In real life there are no *Groundhog Day* do-overs where the painful interaction is conveniently wiped out. As we discussed in chapter 7, memories of our history don't always serve us well.

The debriefing *may* happen at the end of the discussion. This helps you review it with the clearest recall. This is most easily done if you steer clear of discord and damage, and no one is limping or wounded.

Sometimes you've made peace, but it was hard won and you're emotionally spent. Make a commitment to debrief later and agree to a specific time. Follow through! Valuable discovery can come out of some of the most difficult conflict. Don't waste that opportunity.

Make it right with the kids. We raised our sons in modest-sized homes. If we were engaged in an *intense moment of fellowship*, they were aware of it. If it began in front of them, we went into our bedroom and closed the door. But even if it started there, they knew when Mom and Dad were fussing at each other. When it was resolved, we called the boys together and let them know all was well; we were good. We explained that we had asked forgiveness from each other and from God as well. We also asked them to forgive us for troubling the peace in the house.

They told us many years later it was a process that reassured them we loved each other and them. While it was unpleasant, they did not fear divorce or violence. They understood we had not been Mom and Dad at their best, but they knew we were committed to becoming our best.

And we aren't suggesting we've arrived. We still have our moments. Two years ago on a family vacation with our sons and their families, Ron and I exchanged cross words on our way to an amusement park. Everyone was uncomfortable and what should have been be a fun day began with tension. As we continued the quiet bickering from the parking lot to the entrance, one of our sons pulled us aside to remind us of the impact on the entire group; it wasn't just about us. He was right. (Must have had a great set of parents to teach him so well!) We quickly resolved it and called the group together and asked their forgiveness. They were eager to give it and we had a great day.

We were quick to respond to our son because he wasn't making rules *for* us. He was reminding us of our commitments, and it was all we needed to shift our approach. Kind of like a wake-up call or the smelling salts after a sharp blow: that's the power of fighting fair. The rules represent your desire to honor each other and your covenant. When you stray from that approach, the rules or agreements guide you to safe territory.

You'll find a list of the rules in the resource section at the back of this book. They can be helpful in the debriefing. Use them to assess "How'd we do?" and "What can we do the next time conflict comes calling to create a more positive approach to deal with it?"

So let's put on the gloves and fight fair as we head into the final round.

PUT ON THE GLOVES! CHAPTER 8

If possible, we recommend both spouses complete this entire section. Respond to the questions individually, and then come together for a discussion. If you are completing this process alone, record your thoughts to the questions and use the conversation starters for a discussion with your spouse. Record what each of you shares in the "He said / She said" section.

1. What rules or guidelines do you currently have in place for dealing with conflict? They may be unspoken, but understood. How well are they serving you?

2. Which situations could you relate to in this chapter? What rules stood out as potential lifelines for your marriage? Why?

HE SAID / SHE SAID

Use these questions to build a discussion with your spouse. Then each enter your thoughts in a "He Said / She Said" section of your journal.

- How would our relationship be better if we chose to fight fair? What issues still exist because we've been unable or unwilling to discuss them positively and productively?
- What might get in the way of our using the guidelines from this chapter? Which rules will we begin to establish and agree upon? What additional rules might be helpful for us?

GOD SAID

Read these passages of Scripture and discuss.

"Love is patient, love is kind, it isn't jealous, it doesn't brag, it isn't arrogant, it isn't rude, it doesn't seek its own advantage, it isn't irritable, it doesn't keep a record of complaints, it isn't happy with injustice, but it is happy with the truth" (1 Corinthians 13:4-6).

"Let the words of my mouth
  and the meditations of my heart
  be pleasing to you,
  LORD, my rock and my redeemer."
(Psalm 19:14)

"But the fruit of the Spirit is love, joy, peace, patience, kindness, goodness, faithfulness, gentleness, and self-control. There is no law against things like this. Those who belong to Christ Jesus have crucified the self with its passions and its desires. If we live by the Spirit, let's follow the Spirit. Let's not become arrogant, make each other angry, or be jealous of each other" (Galatians 5:22-26).

NEW DISCOVERIES / HOW CAN WE USE THIS INFORMATION?

Be specific! Write in your journal what stands out to you from this chapter.

PRAYER

Father, thank you for loving us and caring about us as individuals and as a couple. We commit to your Word as the blueprint for our married life. We will choose peace and refuse to allow the little things to become the fuel for our conflict. When serious issues arise, our goal is to honor the agreements we've chosen so they support and serve our unity. Please forgive us for living according to our selfish desires without considering the consequences to our children, our extended family, or to how effectively we represent you in our marriage. Thank you for your Son, Jesus, who sacrificed His life for ours. Help us demonstrate our gratitude for His love, His grace, and His sacrifice every day by offering those same things to each other. We thank you for your love.

CHAPTER 9

How Do We Get There from Here?

"Can two people walk together without agreeing on the direction?" (Amos 3:3 NLT).

We can all easily answer this, because we've all attempted it at one time or another. It's not possible to achieve, but it doesn't keep us from trying, and oftentimes arguing about it.

Remember that conflict can be a tremendous asset to your life as husband and wife. Aligning with the Scripture is essential. But beyond that, is there room for more than one perspective, idea, or opinion in a marriage? There'd better be! Or the one idea you have between the two of you had better be fabulous.

Ron and I are wired very differently. He's an engineer; math is a foreign language to me. I don't get it. He sees a side of things I don't unless someone guides me. The opposite is also true: I'm aware of words in a way that sometimes frustrates Ron, because I'm rather precise about them. But as his ministry has grown over the years, he has discovered the power of language and requested my help in his work. We're different. And it works for us. Here's an example of how our differences allow us to walk together in full agreement.

As we stood in our very first home among the boxes on moving day, Ron asked, "Where do you want the couch?" I had given it a lot of thought previously and pointed to the wall where it should go. I also rattled off directions about the other major pieces of furniture and their placement.

"Okay. I'll set it up, just like that. When we've had a chance to see it, I want to arrange it a bit differently. I think it will create a better flow. If you don't like it, I'll return it to your original design right away."

I will admit, I snickered a bit. *Really, now? I'm the woman. I've got the design ideas, but I'll humor him.* "Sure, that sounds great." I was confident in my taste.

He tugged and pushed and pulled and placed the heavy pieces to create the room arrangement I had envisioned. I liked it. A little tight near the dining room door, but overall, it worked.

Then Ron rearranged the furniture to show me his preferred design. I was floored. It was *so* much better.

He didn't need to move it back. We lived there twenty years, and while we replaced the pieces, the arrangement remained the same.

It annoyed me briefly that day, but I've come to trust him. God has gifted him in those areas. He returns the favor because he knows I'm acting in my own giftings.

It was conflict, but we didn't argue. It turned out to be an important moment of *discovery*. There is enormous value in hearing and respecting each other's thoughts and opinions. They are a reflection of who God made us to be. Add in the talents, experience, and abilities you each possess and you have a great place from which to build an extraordinary life.

We're In This Together

Our plan is to draw heavily on the qualities and quirks of the unique individuals God created each of us to be. We refuse to attempt a major makeover on each other. If there's shaping to do, let God do it. Pray for it in yourself and pray for it in your mate. Don't wait until there's an issue, but petition God daily to help each of you become more like Him. He's capable of the makeover. We are not.

This is an essential concept: learn to appreciate and value the unique person you call *spouse*. We use the awareness of our varying strengths to our advantage, and they are baked into the commitments we've made to each other. God has stretched each of us to work beyond our natural strengths (our comfort zones) over the years, but it's usually a temporary assignment.

The plan reminds us of our commitments when we are tempted to splurge on a major purchase in a moment of "Oh my goodness! Did you see what a great deal this is?" Time is another limited resource, so we work on the calendar together to allow for the high priority activities. We've also learned to let go of a lot of the *entitlement thinking* in life: *You work hard; you should get a new car* or *You deserve that spa vacation; you should go ahead and reserve it. Ron will understand.*

We don't live a spartan life, but we aren't extravagant—unless it's one of our Big Rocks that year. We'll discuss the concept of Big Rocks later in this chapter.

So, what are the next steps?

We've laid the groundwork in previous chapters. You have what you need—spiritual, emotional, and practical. The Scriptures have been examined, the baggage unpacked. We have explored tips, tools, and strategies to change the process *and* the outcome for the conflict you encounter. But our prayer is that you don't stop there, set the book aside, and say, "That was helpful. I learned some important stuff." If that's your approach, don't expect any change as a result of the time you invested in reading the chapters.

Knowing the information is great, but it's of no value unless you *do* something with it. If you don't like where you are, move. You are not a tree.

When we know what the Word says and understand what God directs us to do, He expects us to act on it. He holds us accountable to what we know. It's called *obedience*. He doesn't demand perfection immediately, but He is clear: "Let your heart hold on to my words: Keep my commands and live" (Proverbs 4:4). That's a marvelous promise, and it's apparent in the statement that when we do our part, God does His.

He also wants to make it perfectly understood there's another side to the coin. Luke carries that message to us:

> Why do you call me, "Lord, Lord," and do not do what I say? As for everyone who comes to me and hears my words and puts them into practice, I will show you what they are like. They are like a man building a house, who dug down deep and laid the foundation on rock. When a flood came, the torrent struck that house but could not shake it, because it was well built. (Luke 6:46-48 NIV)

If you're not familiar with the less attractive options in this passage, read the rest of the chapter to get the skinny on what happens when we hear but do nothing. Not a pretty sight.

If you've experienced the flood—times you were uncertain your house would stand—God's words are the lifeline He throws us.

First Steps

Where to start?

Our first recommendation is to dig into the Word. Remember, one of the most important foundational rules is to accept Scripture as the blueprint of your life. You've read and discussed chapters filled with Scripture to inscribe on your heart and act on each day. For your convenience, we've included the Scriptures in the resource section of the book. We encourage you to declare them over your marriage. Saying them aloud, together if possible, reinforces your agreement with God's Word in your life and your marriage. Paul calls God's Word the "sword of the Spirit" in Ephesians 6:17. It, along with the rest of the full armor, equips us to turn back the attack of the enemy. Take God's sword into the fight, and the contest is over!

The results of the surveys and interviews with couples who shared their experiences, added to our own, revealed an important observation: much of what causes conflict is the lack of a plan. When couples make it up as they go along (decisions, actions, commitments), they often bump up against each other and the potential for conflict is present. It's easy to feel left out or minimized when your spouse makes a decision in the moment without consulting you. If there's no strategy, no previously discussed and agreed-upon plan or approach, chances increase that you will face problems down the line.

Few of us would start a cross-country vacation with a group of friends without deciding on the route. Those involved in the journey might have ideas or preferences they'd like to discuss. A trip from Los Angeles to New York is filled with options and possibilities. Which route? Where will we stay? What attractions would we like to see? How will we split the cost? Will we stay in four-star hotels or in hostels along the way?

Can you imagine the chaos of that trip with no plan? Constant bickering. Hurt feelings. Major upsets, and then somebody decides, "I'm done. I'm taking the bus home."

With no one in the metaphorical "driver's seat," there's a problem.

Who's in the driver's seat in your marriage? I get a kick out of the bumper sticker (or country song, can't remember which) that says, "Jesus is my copilot." Um, no. There *is* a country song entitled, "Jesus, Take the Wheel." That's more like it. When you put a plan together as husband and wife, with Jesus at the wheel, you will arrive safely at your destination. Creating a plan is our second recommendation.

Sharpen Your Tools

Tools for planning are essential, and few of us had them on our wedding day. You may have developed some over the years; use what works and continue to build on them. Ron and I were married for nearly thirty years before we discovered the power of creating an actual written plan. A little tardy to that party, but what a difference it's made for us. We have two tools we use for the process:

- *Got Vision?* This is a vision planner I created to plan the "big picture" for our life together. We created the original about ten years ago, and we review and update it annually.
- *Big Rocks.* This is the annual plan we create each January.

You can download the complete template for *Got Vision?* at www.debdearmond.com. It comes with a full set of directions, but it's simple to use. Ron and I are not complex people; we didn't want a complex planning process. The first few pages of the vision planner is included as appendix C of this book. It gives you an idea how the process works and explains the value of creating a shared vision.

Here's a bit of a sneak peak. It's taken from the introductory remarks on the cover of the planner itself.

> If you don't know where you're going, any path will do.
>
> You're going to end up somewhere. But will it be what you had hoped for when you married and what God has designed for your life together? Step out of the "let's see where this goes" mode and create a clear statement of purpose for your life as husband and wife.
>
> Inside you will find tools to help light your path to clarity and definition. Define your purpose now.
>
> Habakkuk 2:2—"Then the LORD answered me, and said, 'Write a vision, and make it plain upon a tablet so that a runner can read it.'"

When we created our vision plan ten years ago, we were in the middle of major change. Lifelong Californians, we had just moved to Texas. In those early months it was a little like landing on Mars. It took a while to get used to the drawl and the highway system and the pace of life we have since grown to love. We were without our family, longtime friends, our home church, and everything familiar (and comforting) to us. No support system but God and each other.

Turns out it was all we needed. Oh! And a really good plan made it possible.

We took a weekend away, which seems silly for empty-nesters, but the change of location helped us focus. We had each reviewed the sections beforehand, making a few notes, and then spent the two-and-a-half days together combining, amending, and creating our plan. It includes personal goals for our marriage, as well as personal objectives for each of us individually. We defined objectives for our role as parents, even though none of our children still lived at home. Spiritual goals as well as professional goals were included.

Each year, in early January, we spend time away to review the vision plan (big picture) and update it as God leads. It's been tremendously helpful through the years, serving as our North Star, cheering us on as we make progress. Watching the dreams become reality has built our faith in amazing ways, reminding us how much God loves us and cares about our lives. We serve a good, good Father.

First Things First

During that annual getaway, we also create our Big Rocks plan.

If you are unfamiliar with Stephen Covey's Big Rocks concept, you can view a quick YouTube video that explains it to you. You will find the link in the resources at the back of the book. We suggest you watch together with your spouse, even if you have seen or read about it at some previous time. Viewing it together will help cement the Big Rocks concept.

The summary of the concept is simple: time is a limited resource and we are best served when we spend it wisely. There are multiple demands for our time every day, and the secret to achieve the life God desires for us is to spend our time and energy on the most important things *first*. These are the priorities related to major life concerns, including the big three: faith, family, and career or calling. These are called the *Big Rocks*. These priorities provide a high return on your time, as they help you achieve your vision. Consider them the *must-dos*. You may have additional items on your list, but remember if everything's a priority, nothing is.

Life also includes additional interests and opportunities we view as important, but must be lower on our list of priorities. When it comes to how and where we spend our time and energy, they are considered the *nice-to-dos*. Examples include hobbies, sports, socializing with friends, and community events or volunteering for a local charity. These activities enhance our lives and are almost always enjoyable, but Covey calls them the *Little Rocks*.

Last on the list are those demands that may be urgent—time sensitive or pressing—but they represent busywork, distractions, or trivial activities. They provide a low return for your time and energy. These might include surfing the Web, dealing with junk mail (real and electronic), or spending time with people you don't care for (or who bring you down as a result of being with them). This is the *Sand*. Some of it might be necessary, but our temptation is to do these items first as our day gets under way. Why? They are the *have-to-dos*. We want to get them done quickly and move on to more important commitments and tasks awaiting us. But the Sand always sucks up far more time and energy than we expect it will. And the return is often minimal.

The video depicts the impossibility of getting to the important activities if we first give our time, focus, and energy to the low priorities—the Sand. If we attend to the Big Rocks first, making them our priorities, we can ultimately fit in all the others as well.

One of the bonuses we discovered is that given a bit of time, distractions and busywork will sometimes disappear on their own. If you are not the first to respond when your son's first grade teacher e-mails for cookies for Friday's party, someone else will step in. Should you ignore it every time? Of course not, but many of us believe *If I don't do it, no one else will.* Rubbish. That's a sense of self-importance that can lead to martyr or victim mentality: "I'm the only one who can do this" or "I'm always the one who has to step in at the last minute." The life of a hero is zero and the victim eventually resents the assumption: "Gina will do it. She always says yes. Don't even bother phoning anyone else."

Be discriminating about giving your time away. Invest it instead. Learn to say no. Give your calendar to God and watch what He does with it. A plan created together as a couple, bathed in prayer, including God and the Word, will provide keen awareness of where to spend your time.

In the resource section you will find links to the electronic version of our Big Rocks plan. Adapt it to fit your preferences or needs. We review ours monthly and adjust it as needed. It requires agreement to change it. I (Deb) take incredible delight in checking off the accomplishments. We enjoy discussing the steps we took or the Scripture that empowered our success. It's always a time for reflection on God's presence in our life.

We live in a fast-paced and demanding world. We are connected twenty-four hours a day, seven days a week. Our calendars and planners are overstuffed with events and commitments that can pull our time and attention away from those activities that matter most. Which ones matter most? Those that move us toward achieving our goals and include faith, marriage, family, finances, and career / calling commitments. Without a clear plan and specific goals, we have little hope of building the life God desires for us.

You've got some work to do! Let's get you in the groove with the final *Put on the Gloves!* worksheet.

PUT ON THE GLOVES! CHAPTER 9

If possible, we recommend both spouses complete this entire section. Respond to the questions individually, and then come together for a discussion. If you are completing this process alone, record your thoughts to the questions and use the conversation starters for a discussion with your spouse. Record what each of you shares in the "He said / She said" section.

1. What decision-making tools or plans have you and your mate used in the past? How effective were they in helping you steer clear of conflict, or deal with it constructively?

2. On a scale of 1–10 (1 = low / 10 = high), how much clarity do you and your spouse have about your Big Rocks—the important priorities of your life? What's the impact?

HE SAID / SHE SAID

Use these questions to build a discussion with your spouse. Then each enter your thoughts in a "He Said / She Said" section of your journal.

- What are your thoughts about creating a written plan? What benefit might it be?
- What challenges will you need to deal with to create a plan? What might get in the way?

GOD SAID

Read these passages of Scripture and discuss.

- "Can two people walk together without agreeing on the direction?" (Amos 3:3 NLT).

- "When there's no vision, the people get out of control, but whoever obeys instruction is happy" (Proverbs 29:18).

New Discoveries / How Can We Use This Information?

Be specific! Write in your journal what stands out to you from this chapter.

Prayer

Father, thank you for giving us the power of your Word so we can know and understand your plans for us. We give you full access to our relationship and desire to follow no plan but the one you have designed for us. Our goal is to align our lives as husband and wife with your will, your Word, and your ways. We will not pursue our own selfish ambitions, but we will work to honor each other, prefer each other over ourselves, and always work with the best interest of our mate in mind. Please support us with the self-discipline and commitment we will need to create a vision and a plan for our lives. Help us follow through, regardless of our previous starts and failures. You are a good, good Father, desiring the best for us, and the best for us is to stay the course and follow through. Please guide us as we move together in the blessing of agreement.

APPENDIX A

Scriptures and Intentions

This section is designed to support you as you pursue the marriage you (and God) desire. For the Christ follower, that means building a life together based on the Scriptures. Here you will find a chapter-by-chapter listing of the passages in the book.

Along with listing the Scriptures, we have created an intention for each chapter based on the Word of God. An intention is defined as a goal, plan, or purpose—and goals based on Scripture will always have God's support!

Declaring your intention establishes it in your heart. There are several options to use the intentions:

- Include them when you pray, either individually or as a couple.
- Review and declare them during your regular vision plan discussions.
- Bring them to difficult conversations as a reminder of the commitments and rewards that come from honoring them.

- Create a list and choose one for each week as a reminder of your promise to each other (and God).

Introduction

INTENTION

We are not enemies, but allies, and will not turn on each other. We join forces against the authorities of this world that are determined to destroy our marriage, our family, and us. We treat conflict as an opportunity for discovery that benefits our union, rather than as an opening for damage and destruction.

SCRIPTURE

"For we are not fighting against flesh-and-blood enemies, but against evil rulers and authorities of the unseen world, against mighty powers in this dark world, and against evil spirits in the heavenly places." (Ephesians 6:12 NLT)

Chapter 1

INTENTION

We are not controlled by anger and refuse to allow the devil to have any place in our life together. We release anger swiftly and forgive quickly. Our heavenly Father will bless us as we stand in agreement on the truth found in His Word.

SCRIPTURE

"And 'don't sin by letting anger control you.' Don't let the sun go down while you are still angry, for anger gives a foothold to the devil." (Ephesians 4:26-27 NLT)

"Again I assure you that if two of you agree on earth about anything you ask, then my Father who is in heaven will do it for you." (Matthew 18:19)

Chapter 2

INTENTION

We press forward together in Christ, pursuing His kingdom and each other because our marriage is worth fighting for. As a result, our life together is victorious.

SCRIPTURE

"Since we are surrounded by so great a cloud of witnesses, let us lay aside every weight, and the sin which so easily ensnares us, and let us run with endurance the race that is set before us." (Hebrews 12:1 NKJV)

"But in all these things we win a sweeping victory through the one who loved us." (Romans 8:37)

Chapter 3

INTENTION

Godly wisdom is not found in our experiences or thoughts, but in knowing and understanding the Word and character of the Lord. Only through the Word can we enjoy emotional health and balance. We rely on the Scriptures and the operation of His Spirit to teach us to love without conditions and walk in wisdom.

SCRIPTURE

"This is how everyone will know that you are my disciples, when you love each other." (John 13:35)

"Get wisdom! / Get understanding before anything else." (Proverbs 4:7)

"The beginning of wisdom is the fear of the LORD; / the knowledge of the holy one is understanding." (Proverbs 9:10)

"But anyone who needs wisdom should ask God, whose very nature is to give to everyone without a second thought, without keeping score. Wisdom will certainly be given to those who ask." (James 1:5)

Chapter 4

INTENTION

Words matter and we use them wisely to build our relationship, not destroy each other. We speak the truth in love and listen to each other respectfully. We receive wisdom from God, who gives it to all who ask.

SCRIPTURE

"Submit to each other out of respect for Christ." (Ephesians 5:21)

"Fools see their own way as right, / but the wise listen to advice." (Proverbs 12:15)

"A word out of your mouth may seem of no account, but it can accomplish nearly anything—or destroy it!" (James 3:5 *THE MESSAGE*)

"For the word of God is alive and powerful. It is sharper than the sharpest two-edged sword, cutting between soul and spirit, between joint and marrow. It exposes our innermost thoughts and desires." (Hebrews 4:12 NLT)

"I listen to their conversations
   and don't hear a word of truth.
Is anyone sorry for doing wrong?
   Does anyone say, 'What a terrible thing I have done'?
No! All are running down the path of sin
   as swiftly as a horse galloping into battle!" (Jeremiah 8:6 NLT)

"Let your conversation be gracious and attractive so that you will have the right response for everyone." (Colossians 4:6 NLT)

Chapter 5

INTENTION

We are equipped with divine weapons that allow us to overcome every temptation—unbelief, anger, and every stronghold—through Christ who has made us new. We thank you that you have created us as unique individuals and seek to merge our styles so that we manage conflict in a productive way.

SCRIPTURE

"When they finished eating, Jesus asked Simon Peter, 'Simon son of John, do you love me more than these?'

Simon replied, 'Yes, Lord, you know I love you.'

Jesus said to him, 'Feed my lambs.' Jesus asked a second time, 'Simon son of John, do you love me?'

Simon replied, 'Yes, Lord, you know I love you.'

Jesus said to him, 'Take care of my sheep.' He asked a third time, 'Simon son of John, do you love me?'

Peter was sad that Jesus asked him a third time, 'Do you love me?' He replied, 'Lord, you know everything; you know I love you.'

Jesus said to him, 'Feed my sheep.'" (John 21:15-17)

"Hotheads stir up conflict,

but patient people calm down strife." (Proverbs 15:18)

"This means that anyone who belongs to Christ has become a new person. The old life is gone; a new life has begun!" (2 Corinthians 5:17 NLT)

"No temptation has overtaken you except what is common to humanity. God is faithful, and He will not allow you to be tempted beyond what you are able, but with the temptation He will also provide a way of escape so that you are able to bear it." (1 Corinthians 10:13 HCSB)

"The weapons we fight with are not the weapons of the world. On the contrary, they have divine power to demolish strongholds." (2 Corinthians 10:4 NIV)

Chapter 6

INTENTION

We are transformed by the renewing of our minds through study of the Scripture, clear about what God's will is for our life, our marriage, and our family. We strive for the communication skills that bring peace and build each other up. We don't behave childishly but walk as mature believers in Christ, serving each other before self. We let the Spirit renew our thoughts and attitudes, developing us as children of the day, truthful, holy, and righteous through Christ who died for us.

SCRIPTURE

"Don't do anything for selfish purposes, but with humility think of others as better than yourselves. Instead of each person watching out for their own good, watch out for what is better for others." (Philippians 2:3-4)

"No one should look out for their own advantage, but they should look out for each other." (1 Corinthians 10:24)

"You will not enter and occupy the land I swore to give you. The only exceptions will be Caleb son of Jephunneh and Joshua son of Nun." (Numbers 14:30 NLT)

"When I was a child, I used to speak like a child, reason like a child, think like a child. But now that I have become a man, I've put an end to childish things." (1 Corinthians 13:11)

"But I say to you that everyone who is angry with their brother or sister will be in danger of judgment. If they say to their brother or sister, 'You idiot,' they will be in danger of being condemned by the governing council. And if they say, 'You fool,' they will be in danger of fiery hell." (Matthew 5:22)

"Then we will no longer be immature like children. We won't be tossed and blown about by every wind of new teaching. We will not be influenced when people try to trick us with lies so clever they sound like the truth. Instead, we will speak the truth in love, growing in every way more and more like Christ, who is the head of his body, the church." (Ephesians 4:14-15 NLT)

"When he lies, it is consistent with his character; for he is a liar and the father of lies." (John 8:44 NLT)

"So let's strive for the things that bring peace and the things that build each other up." (Romans 14:19)

"All of you are children of light and children of the day. We don't belong to night or darkness." (1 Thessalonians 5:5)

"Since you have heard about Jesus and have learned the truth that comes from him, throw off your old sinful nature and your former way of life, which is corrupted by lust and deception. Instead, let the Spirit renew your thoughts and attitudes. Put on your new nature, created to be like God—truly righteous and holy." (Ephesians 4:21-24 NLT)

"Don't be conformed to the patterns of this world, but be transformed by the renewing of your minds so that you can figure out what God's will is—what is good and pleasing and mature." (Romans 12:2)

"A gentle answer deflects anger, / but harsh words make tempers flare." (Proverbs 15:1 NLT)

"What is the source of conflict among you? What is the source of your disputes? Don't they come from your cravings that are at war in your own lives? You long for something you don't have, so you commit murder. You are jealous for something you can't get, so you struggle and fight. You don't have because you don't ask. You ask and don't have because you ask with evil intentions, to waste it on your own cravings." (James 4:1-3)

"Do all things without murmurings and disputings: That ye may be blameless and harmless, the sons of God, without rebuke, in the midst of a crooked and perverse nation, among whom ye shine as lights in the world; Holding forth the word of life; that I may rejoice in the day of Christ, that I have not run in vain, neither laboured in vain." (Philippians 2:14-16 KJV)

"Know this, my dear brothers and sisters: everyone should be quick to listen, slow to speak, and slow to grow angry. This is because an angry person doesn't produce God's righteousness. Therefore, with humility, set aside all moral filth and the growth of wickedness, and welcome the word planted deep inside you—the very word that is able to save you. You must be doers of the word and not only hearers who mislead themselves." (James 1:19-22)

Chapter 7

INTENTION

We are united, one flesh, stuck together like glue! Nothing, no one, not even we ourselves, will pull us apart. Our unity is protected as we draw near to God and His Word, refusing to retaliate or use revenge when we are hurt or feel wronged by each other. We will honor our relationship, which will bring honor to God.

SCRIPTURE

"So they are no longer two but one flesh." (Matthew 19:6)

"Therefore, humans must not pull apart what God has put together." (Mark 10:9)

"Never pay back evil with more evil. Do things in such a way that everyone can see you are honorable." (Romans 12:17 NLT)

"Don't pay back evil for evil or insult for insult. Instead, give blessing in return. You were called to do this so that you might inherit a blessing." (1 Peter 3:9)

"Don't say, 'I'll do to them what they did to me. / I'll pay them back for their actions.'" (Proverbs 24:29)

"When they hurled their insults at him, he did not retaliate; when he suffered, he made no threats. Instead, he entrusted himself to him who judges justly." (1 Peter 2:23 NIV)

"But I say to you, love your enemies, bless those who curse you, do good to those who hate you, and pray for those who spitefully use you and persecute you, that you may be sons of your Father in heaven;

for He makes His sun rise on the evil and on the good, and sends rain on the just and on the unjust. For if you love those who love you, what reward have you? Do not even the tax collectors do the same? And if you greet your brethren only, what do you do more than others? Do not even the tax collectors do so?" (Matthew 5:44-47 NKJV)

"[Love] doesn't keep a record of complaints." (1 Corinthians 13:5)

"Be tolerant with each other and, if someone has a complaint against anyone, forgive each other. As the Lord forgave you, so also forgive each other." (Colossians 3:13)

"Therefore, submit to God. Resist the devil, and he will run away from you. Come near to God, and he will come near to you." (James 4:7-8)

"For we are not fighting against flesh-and-blood enemies, but against evil rulers and authorities of the unseen world, against mighty powers in this dark world, and against evil spirits in the heavenly places." (Ephesians 6:12 NLT)

Chapter 8

INTENTION

We choose life in Christ, as it is the only successful way to live. We seek instruction from God's Word as it provides the key to success in our marriage, our family, and all we do. We live in peace, without stumbling, because we choose life in Christ and God's Word to direct our actions, behaviors, decisions, and thoughts.

SCRIPTURE

"We demolish arguments and every pretension that sets itself up against the knowledge of God, and we take captive every thought to make it obedient to Christ." (2 Corinthians 10:5 NIV)

"Every scripture is inspired by God and is useful for teaching, for showing mistakes, for correcting, and for training character." (2 Timothy 3:16)

"The people who love your Instruction enjoy peace—and lots of it. / There's no stumbling for them!" (Psalm 119:165)

"My people are destroyed
  from lack of knowledge.
Since you have rejected knowledge,
  so I will reject you from serving me as a priest.
Since you have forgotten the Instruction of your God,
  so also I will forget your children." (Hosea 4:6)

"If it is possible, as far as it depends on you, live at peace with everyone." (Romans 12:18 NIV)

"And among all the parts of the body, the tongue is a flame of fire. It is a whole world of wickedness, corrupting your entire body. It can set your whole life on fire, for it is set on fire by hell itself." (James 3:6 NLT)

"A person's wisdom yields patience;
  it is to one's glory to overlook an offense." (Proverbs 19:11 NIV)

"Love is patient, love is kind, it isn't jealous, it doesn't brag, it isn't arrogant, it isn't rude, it doesn't seek its own advantage, it isn't irritable, it doesn't keep a record of complaints, it isn't happy with injustice, but it is happy with the truth." (1 Corinthians 13:4-6)

"Let the words of my mouth
  and the meditations of my heart
  be pleasing to you,
  LORD, my rock and my redeemer." (Psalm 19:14)

"But the fruit of the Spirit is love, joy, peace, patience, kindness, goodness, faithfulness, gentleness, and self-control. There is no law against things like this. Those who belong to Christ Jesus have crucified the self with its passions and its desires.

If we live by the Spirit, let's follow the Spirit. Let's not become arrogant, make each other angry, or be jealous of each other." (Galatians 5:22-26)

Chapter 9

INTENTION

We believe God has a rock solid plan for our life together. Through prayer and study of His Word, we will understand His specific vision and purpose for us. As we submit to His direction, He will guide us to create plans for achieving our God-inspired goals together. As we build our house on the solid rock that is the Word, it will stand against anything that might come against us.

SCRIPTURE

"Can two people walk together / without agreeing on the direction?" (Amos 3:3 NLT)

"Let your heart hold on to my words: / Keep my commands and live." (Proverbs 4:4)

"Why do you call me, 'Lord, Lord,' and do not do what I say? As for everyone who comes to me and hears my words and puts them into practice, I will show you what they are like. They are like a man building a house, who dug down deep and laid the foundation on rock. When a flood came, the torrent struck that house but could not shake it, because it was well built." (Luke 6:46-48 NIV)

"When there's no vision, the people get out of control, / but whoever obeys instruction is happy." (Proverbs 29:18)

"Then the LORD answered me and said,

Write a vision, and make it plain upon a tablet

so that a runner can read it."

(Habbakuk 2:2)

APPENDIX B

THE RULES

Use this list as a quick reference. You can also use it as a checklist to identify where you are currently on solid footing. Leverage the benefit of these guidelines by using them consistently. Identify those behaviors that are not used or used often. These indicate opportunity to develop improved patterns that will support constructive conversations when differences arise.

The Foundational Agreements: Before an Issue Arises

- The Word of God is the blueprint for our life as believers.
- Not in front of the kids.
- Don't use the *D* word.
- Exclude violence.

Approach: As You Enter the Discussion

- Pray.
- Timing is everything.

- Both partners will actively work toward peace.
- If it's not a big deal, don't make it a big deal.
- Touch.

Discover: Explore and Discuss

- No clairvoyance allowed.
- "What did you say?"
- Clean up after yourself.
- Collaborate and partner together.
- Stay on track.
- Stay out of the weeds.
- Lighten up!

Challenges: In the Heat of the Moment

- Avoid the absolutes.
- Don't interrupt.
- Don't make threats.

Back on Track: When the Dust Settles

- Pray together.
- Debrief.
- Make it right with the kids.

APPENDIX C

EXCERPT FROM *GOT VISION?*

If you don't know where you're going, any path will do. You will end up *somewhere*. But will that be where you wanted to go? More importantly, is it the race God has chosen for you and your spouse to run together?

Moving forward as one is much trickier than doing it solo! Remember those three-legged races we ran as kids? It requires patience, focus, and concentration to coordinate the unity required to make it to the finish line together. So here are a few things to think about:

- A goal without a deadline is just a dream. If you want to live your dream and fulfill God's purpose for your lives, you must choose to do so. God has a dream and a future for you. Finding it is a matter of prayer and commitment to pursue his plan. The only path to success it to make the choice to do so—together.
- Achieving your dream requires work, but is far less difficult when you are focused, have a plan, and can agree on where you're going and how you will get there.
- Defining your desired life outcomes and identifying the

steps required to achieve it helps ensure that you move deliberately toward those goals.

- Once you've given thought to what you want to do and how you want to do it, you will find that your choices are more directed and your decisions are made with greater confidence.

- Life is a choice. Many make their choices by default. Not choosing *is* a choice and it leaves you without focus, direction, or foundations to support a happily ever after.

- Lastly, writing it down makes it real. It gives you a tool to measure your progress. And life with a plan in hand is better than hoping for the best by making it up as you go along!

Vision, Mission, and Values—Which Comes First?

Business writer Ryan Rieches asked "What Comes First Vision or Mission?" He wrote, "Here is an easy way to remember—Just put ARY at the end of each. For example: A visionARY is one who sees into the future and can visualize a clear destination. A missionARY is one who helps realize that vision." In other words: "A vision statement answers—WHAT do we aim to achieve? A mission statement answers—HOW do we plan to achieve this vision?"

For couples, the addition of our values helps us identify the paths, boundaries, and signposts that we want to honor as we make the journey.

While this plan is designed to be used by couples, to establish your vision, mission, and values, you may find pieces can be useful individually. You can use this same exercise to create goals specific to your career or other roles you fill. Remember, however, that those must be aligned with your plan as husband and wife, which always comes first.

Step 1: Creating a Vision and Values Statement for Your Marriage

Start by identifying the values you wish to honor as a couple and demonstrate in your life together. Make a list of as many as come to your minds as important values. Once it's completed, identify the 10 that are closest to your heart. Review and then together rank them from 1 to 10, with 1 being the most important in your life. Finally, select the top 5 as those you will include in your statement. Define what these values mean to you.

OUR CORE VALUES
These values are not negotiable in our life; they serve to guide our choices, our behavior, and our decisions. We will strive to live them consistently every day.

[Writing space is available in the actual template, which is available for download at www.debdearmond.com.]

You are now ready to draft your vision statement. Approach writing your vision statement with a prayerful heart. Ask God to guide your thoughts and reveal his will as you meditate about the direction of your life.

Use the questions on the next page to help focus your vision statement. Answer each question as completely and honestly as possible. Add other questions and answers if they come to mind. Remember to check responses to align with the values you have identified.

Personal Vision Statement Template

You will start by answering questions that will build a vision statement—a brief expression of what it is you want to become as a couple and fulfill what God desires for your life as husband and wife. If you have children, include them as you think through the questions. Think of it as the "big picture." Use the questions below to identify the components that will make up your vision statement. Be honest with yourselves, think through each one carefully and record your responses. (All of these questions include writing space in the template, which is available for download at www.debdearmond .com.)

- Who are we? What are the things we believe and actively seek to demonstrate in our marriage, our home, our family relationships? What about in our church, in our community, and on the job? What role does faith play in our lives?
- What purpose(s) do we believe God has called us to fulfill? Together and individually?
- What are we passionate about? What are the things that bring us joy?
- How would we live our lives if time and resources were not an issue?
- What are the habits we need to form in order to be successful individually and as a couple? As husband and wife, mom and dad? What will we need to form as a habit to succeed spiritually?
- What are the patterns that hold us back? What habits do we need to break in our marriage relationship?
- Other areas we want to include in our vision:

Next Steps

Use the responses from the template to create a vision statement. Write about the core values and recurring themes your answers reveal in the following areas:

- spiritual growth and development, including ministry
- family relationships
- friends
- financial health
- professional aspirations
- physical health
- personal growth and development

If some of your answers fall outside of these categories, create your own.

Keep it brief: three to five sentences maximum. Include statements that address:

- What's your ultimate desire for your life together?
- What do you desire to accomplish jointly?
- What's God's direction and calling on your life?
- What is the legacy you hope to achieve?

Think about how you can use information from your past to shape the future. Distill the information in each life category into one or two actionable statements. Write using first-person perspective and present tense. For example, under the spiritual category, you could write, "*I am* deepening my relationship with Christ through Scripture study and prayer" or "*I am* experiencing the joy of drawing others to Christ through love," rather than "*I will.*" Write concrete statements that are based on your core values.

Your Personal Vision Statement

Read your personal vision statement often—perhaps as often as once each week. Review it on Sunday evening to gauge your success in "walking your talk" in the past week and to help set your focus for the coming week. Use it to guide your daily actions and decisions. Over time, you may want to make changes as your circumstances and abilities change.

Once your vision statement is complete and your values are identified, turn your attention to creating a *mission statement*—a plan that will help you accomplish the vision on a day-to-day basis. Use the steps on the next page to guide you.

Step 2: Writing a Personal Mission Statement

A personal mission statement is a brief description of what you want to focus on in order to accomplish your vision. Goals can then be identified for a period of the next one to three years and should be expressed in your mission statement. It is a way to focus your energy, actions, behaviors and decisions toward the things that are most important to you. Think of this as the detailed day-to-day road map.

The first step is creating an outcome for each area of your vision statement. This exercise requires some reflective thinking, so it is best to set some quiet time aside without distractions or interruptions. What steps will you need to take in life to accomplish your vision? What goals will you need to set and pursue actively? Think of your mission as that which powers your vision or makes the vision a reality.

Mission Template

The complete template is available for download at www .debdearmond.com. The first column, "Category," contains the areas you have identified in your vision (personal, professional, spiritual, and so on). Now, in the next column, "Specific Goals," record specific steps, action plan items, and so on that will move you toward achievement of the desired end result.

Step 3: Live Your Vision! Walk It Out!

Congratulations! If you have completed all three steps, you are well on your way to accomplishing your vision. Keep your plan where you can be reminded that this will require a consistent commitment and daily effort. But it *is* worth it.

I encourage you to share your plan with others who are significant in your life and will help to hold you accountable. Good partners are those who will pray for you and encourage you when you are tempted to throw in the towel. We all get discouraged at times. Remember you don't drown by falling into the water. You drown by staying there! Seek help and seek God when you need a lifeline to get back on track.

Remember this is a process to create a joint plan for your lives as a married couple. It is also helpful to use all or parts of the process for creating a plan for each of you, as individuals.

Remember Habakkuk 2:2: "Then the LORD answered me and said, Write a vision, and make it plain upon a tablet so that a runner can read it."

Resources

References

Bacon, Francis. "Of Revenge." In vol. 1 of *The Works of Francis Bacon*. Page 14. Philadelphia: Carey and Hart, 1842.

Chapman, Gary and Jennifer Thomas. *When Sorry Isn't Enough: Making Things Right with Those You Love*, rev. ed. (Chicago: Northfield, 2013).

Cloud, Henry, and John Townsend. *Boundaries in Marriage* (Grand Rapids: Zondervan, 2002).

Cole, Edwin Louis. *Communication, Sex, and Money.* 2nd ed. (Southlake, TX: Watercolor Books, 2002).

Covey, Stephen. *The Seven Habits of Highly Successful People* (New York: Simon & Schuster, 2013).

Ferguson, David and Don McMinn. *Emotional Fitness: Developing a Wholesome Heart* (Irving, TX: Intimacy Press, 2003).

Lawrence, Bill. "Marriage, How IT Works (Genesis 2:18-25)," Bible. org (July 7, 2008), https://bible.org/seriespage/marriage -how-it-works-genesis-218-25.

Rieches, Ryan, "What Comes First Vision or Mission?" Branding Business blog, May 24, 2011, accessed February 12, 2016, www.brandingbusiness.com/blogs/what-comes-first-vision-or-mission.

Runde, Craig, and Tim Flanagan. *Becoming a Conflict Competent Leader: How You and Your Organization Can Manage Conflict Effectively* (San Francisco: Jossey-Bass, 2007). https://nclp.umd.edu/resources/bookreviews/BookReview-Becoming_a_Conflict_Competent_Leader-Draper-2011.pdf.

Schrodt, Paul, Paul L. Witt, and Jenna R. Shimkowski. "A Meta-Analytical Review of the Demand/Withdraw Pattern of Interaction and Its Associations with Individual, Relational, and Communicative Outcomes," *Communication Monographs* 81, no. 1 (2014).

Smalley, Dr. Gary, and Ted Cunningham. *From Anger to Intimacy: How Forgiveness Can Transform Your Marriage* (Grand Rapids: Revell, 2009).

Smith, Alan and Nancy. *Finding the One: Thinking Differently About Choosing a Spouse* (Fort Worth: Authority Press, 2013).

Taylor, Jeremy. *The Sermons of the Right Rev. Jeremy Taylor*. Page 143. Philadelphia: H. Hooker, 1845.

Websites and Tools

EMOTIONALLY HEALTHY SPIRITUALITY ASSESSMENT
http://www.emotionallyhealthy.org/?s=assessment
Free online assessment from emotionallyhealthy.org. This

twenty- to thirty-minute tool was created to help individuals, teams, or churches get a sense of whether their discipleship has touched the emotional components of their lives and, if so, how much. Each stage of emotional maturity is described fully at the end of the assessment.

BIG ROCKS VIDEO LINK

http://bit.ly/1yJqYAA

Video describing Steven Covey's concept of spending time on the important things—the Big Rocks—in life first.

BRAINSTORMING, DECISION-MAKING, AND PROBLEM-SOLVING TOOLS

www.debdearmond.com

My website has many resources available, including the Vision Planner and Big Rocks worksheets.

Made in the USA
Lexington, KY
04 April 2017